Praise for *Money, Manifestation & Miracles*

"A profound and valuable guide to empowering women financially, showing them how to create a tremendous impact on the world while substantially increasing their income."

— **Barbara Stanny,** author of *Sacred Success:*
A Course in Financial Miracles

"The right book at the right time can change your life. *Money, Manifestation & Miracles* is the right book at the right time for a great many people, both women and men. So many of us have been conflicted about money, consciously and subconsciously, and it has prevented us from realizing our full potential and fully realizing our dreams. This book gets to the core of the problem and clearly shows us, step-by-step, how to truly transform our lives not only financially but spiritually and emotionally as well. Meriflor Toneatto's work as a coach and speaker has already changed countless people's lives, and now her book will reach many more. Prepare yourself for some truly remarkable results!"

— **Marc Allen,** author of *Visionary Business* and *The Magical Path*

"We all need assistance in those areas of our lives that challenge us, and finances are one area where a valuable step-by-step guide for transforming and empowering women's relationships with money is needed. *Money, Manifestation & Miracles* is that valuable tool that will assist you in transforming your money stress into financial security. A must-read!"

— **Kristine Carlson,** *New York Times*–bestselling author of
Don't Sweat the Small Stuff for Women and coauthor
(with Richard Carlson) of *Don't Sweat the Small Stuff in Love*

"You can be both spiritual and rich! *Money, Manifestation & Miracles* encourages readers to get over limiting beliefs about money and offers tools to get on with being a 'difference maker' and a force for good in the world."

Cara Bradley, author of
On the Ver

"*Money, Manifestation & Miracles* 1
women in every stage of life. Wl

stay-at-home mom, or a corporate executive, Meriflor Toneatto's principles will help you get aligned for financial success."
— **Joy Chudacoff,** author of *What's Next?: The 7 Steps to Discover Your Big Idea and Create a Wildly Successful Business*

"Meriflor Toneatto shows the dynamic energy exchange between money and soul, spirituality and wealth. To be spiritual and rich at the same time is the core of her message. This book is a catalyst for personal growth and transformation — capturing all the essentials of wealth creation."
— **Tania Gabrielle,** wealth astro-numerologist

"This book shows women how they can be financially independent, flourish in their business and life, and make a big difference in the world socially. Meriflor Toneatto's authenticity and experience help women through the major emotional pitfalls of money. This is a must-read for any woman who wants to move forward past financially limiting beliefs and into a world of financial prosperity."
— **Ruth Klein,** author of *Time Management Secrets for Working Women*

"We are physical beings in a physical universe. Meriflor Toneatto explains that money is the interface between this fact and our as-yet-unmanifest potential. She encourages us to face the fears and doubts that limit our ability to fully realize our immense potential. As a woman, an entrepreneur, an educator, and a coach, I recommend that you read and nourishingly put into action the steps in Meriflor's book."
— **Linda J. Page, PhD,** coauthor (with David Rock) of *Coaching with the Brain in Mind: Foundations for Practice*

"This book takes you on a deeply personal and insightful journey into how you can create a new, empowering relationship with money — and a rich and soul-fulfilling business at the same time. A must-read for every woman."
— **Kendall SummerHawk,** money, marketing, and soul coach

MONEY,
MANIFESTATION *&*
MIRACLES

MONEY,
MANIFESTATION &
MIRACLES

A Guide to Transforming Women's
Relationships with Money

MERIFLOR TONEATTO

Foreword by Ingrid Vanderveldt

New World Library
Novato, California

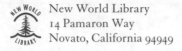

New World Library
14 Pamaron Way
Novato, California 94949

Text design by Tona Pearce Myers

Library of Congress Cataloging-in-Publication Data
Names: Toneatto, Meriflor, [date.]– author.
Title: Money, manifestation & miracles : a guide to transforming women's relationships with money / Meriflor Toneatto ; foreword by Ingrid Vanderveldt.
Other titles: Money, manifestation and miracles
Description: Novato, California : New World Library, [2018] | Includes bibliographical references.
Identifiers: LCCN 2017045320 (print) | LCCN 2017054889 (ebook) | ISBN 9781608685226 (Ebook) | ISBN 9781608685219 (alk. paper)
Subjects: LCSH: Money—Psychological aspects. | Women—Finance, Personal.
Classification: LCC HG222.3 (ebook) | LCC HG222.3 .T66 2018 (print) | DDC 332.0240082—dc23
LC record available at https://lccn.loc.gov/2017045320

First printing, March 2018
ISBN 978-1-60868-521-9
Ebook ISBN 978-1-60868-522-6
Printed in Canada on 100% postconsumer-waste recycled paper

 New World Library is proud to be a Gold Certified Environmentally Responsible Publisher. Publisher certification awarded by Green Press Initiative. www.greenpressinitiative.org

10   9   8   7   6   5   4   3   2   1

Dedicated to you —

claim your wealth, and rise as a force for good.

CONTENTS

Part 3: A Holistic Approach

FOREWORD

Congratulations! You are holding in your hands one of the best books on life, love, business, and money that I have ever read.

In fact, after I read it, filled it with sticky notes, underlined key lessons, earmarked pages, and read it again, I called Meriflor and said, "If there was one book I wish I could write, it is the one that is in my hands. It has truly changed my life."

And I am confident it will change yours too.

Growing up, I thought I would be a missionary. I thought I would help the world in a big way. And I also enjoyed the power that money could bring in terms of helping me make an impact. However, I always struggled with how to bridge the idea that it's okay to do good in the world *and* to make a lot of money. I've spent my life searching for a way to achieve that balance.

This book will show you how it's done — doing what you love while making money — and in my opinion, the approach outlined here is really the only way to do it!

This book will inspire you, bring you hope, and gift you with a mind-set that will bring you abundance in all areas of your life. *Money, Manifestation & Miracles* is *the* book on how women and men look at money differently and how money is a manifestation of a greater spiritual calling.

Meriflor explains how money is love manifested and how love can be money manifested. She brings us to a place that essentially asks the question: "Do you want more love in your life?" If the answer is "yes!" then you can expect to create and have more money as well. That is, if you apply what Meriflor teaches here.

At first you might have a number of thoughts, including, "Oh no, not another book on *manifesting your wealth* without the tools to help get you there" or "money is not love, and love is not money" or "money is money, and love is love." If so, I am here to tell you that Meriflor takes you on a journey — one that meets you wherever you are in your life — a love and money journey, and helps you, in a practical way, to get to the bottom of what drives both.

Why this book and why now?

Maybe you're at a stage in your life where things just aren't where you want or thought they would be. Maybe you are struggling. Maybe you are praying for a signal. Maybe you are hoping for answers.

I know, because I've been there too. I know what it's like to have nothing. Many years ago I lost everything when a company I was developing fell apart and I became broke and homeless. I know what it's like to lose it all and have to rebuild. I know what it's like to be depressed, confused, and hopeless. I've been 100 percent in a place that is *not* helpful in terms of attracting anything — especially abundance and wealth. But I ended up learning vital lessons and paying attention to signals along the way that helped change my mind-set and get me out of that dark place.

Consider your reading this as a signal. This is your book.

Let's fast-forward. On the flip side, I *also* know what it's like to have millions of dollars and find myself in a place where my husband and I looked at each other and asked, "What do we *do* with all this?" We have answered that question. We poured the money into the company I run today, Empowering a Billion Women by 2020 — or EBW2020 for short — to help empower women globally through financial literacy and mentorship. I now know what it's like to be bursting with love, energy, enthusiasm, focus, abundance, and wealth.

But whether you are the CEO of a company, a stay-at-home mother, an entrepreneur, an executive, or an employee, this book has something for you, if you want more love and more money in your world.

When I was led in prayer to start EBW2020, to both follow my calling and make money, that was when I understood what Meriflor so eloquently writes about in this book. True abundance, on any level, comes from within. Doing the inner work *as well as* the outer work is the key to making any dream a reality. When we do this, miracles happen. When I started EBW2020, with the goal to become the number one financial empowerment community for women worldwide, I knew that I needed global experience to reach a wider community.

Shortly thereafter, I found myself as the entrepreneur in residence for Dell, a Fortune 50 company, overseeing entrepreneurial initiatives globally. My *love* was lining up with the money, and the money was lining up with the *love*. Dell realized that to grow its business with entrepreneurs, it was time to help them achieve their dreams by doing what they *love*. Soon I was overseeing a $250 million fund for entrepreneurs. And there it was again — the alignment of love and money — even in a Fortune 50 company.

I first met Meriflor at an EBW2020 event. I saw the importance of what she was teaching, so in our entrepreneurial venture at EBW2020, we have made *Money, Manifestation & Miracles* one of our core recommendations to help women (and men) grow in life, business, love, and money. Meriflor's explanation of the phenomena of love and money shows all of us how to apply this in our own lives too. With this foundational knowledge, anything is possible.

In the end, I simply want to leave you with this: at some point in your life, it will be time to take a deep breath, pause, and give yourself the gift of self-care, love, hope, and more. If you follow what Meriflor teaches in this book, you will not only be gifting all that to yourself, but you will have an inspired plan that I am confident will start attracting money, abundance, and wealth into your life.

I couldn't be more excited that you are holding the key to unlocking your potential and to leaving your gift to the world, whether it be small or a global game changer. Since we as women are increasing our role in creating a global sustainable future for all, this is a perfect time for you to be holding this book in your hands. This book will increase your self-confidence, your contribution, and your impact as you grow to leave your mark on the world.

I wish you joy as you read this book and watch money, manifestation, and miracles start to appear in your life.

— INGRID VANDERVELDT,
Founder and CEO, EBW 2020

INTRODUCTION

I BELIEVE THAT THERE ARE NO COINCIDENCES and that everything unfolds at the exact right time. It is no coincidence that I felt inspired to write this book to help women embrace money, wealth, and abundance as a powerful tool to recognize their greatness, lead a life of significance, and make a positive social impact on the world.

It is also no coincidence that this book has come into your life at this time. You are likely ready to align your talents and passion with your purpose and the meaningful contribution you want to make. You are also likely ready to take action to achieve financial prosperity and success while fulfilling your social promise in the world.

Social promise is your soul's desire to give back by

doing good while doing well in life. It includes a dual goal of combining wealth and profits with a mission to better society. Fulfilling your social promise can be expressed in many ways, such as supporting worthy local or global causes and the issues you most care about.

Your social promise provides a strong motivation for aligning your purpose and passion with service and contribution. Your contributions to others, as a result of your professional endeavors, will allow you not only to change lives but to deeply enrich your own life — as well as your bottom line — beyond your wildest dreams.

Let me ask you this:

What if you truly believed in your own magnificence and ability to step into your greatness and realize your highest potential?

What if you had the courage to extend your limits and create the life of your dreams, one that is rich and fulfilling in every way — financially, spiritually, and emotionally?

What if you had the tools to create a thriving six- or seven-figure income that would allow you to realize financial freedom, have an incredible lifestyle, and make a meaningful difference?

What if I told you that this and more is possible to achieve once you gain a deeper understanding of — and take action on — transforming your relationship with money?

You may be thinking, "How can I have a relationship with money when money is an inanimate object?"

Like it or not, you are in a relationship with anything that preoccupies your time, thoughts, and actions — including money. In fact, the longest relationships that you will have are, first, your relationship with yourself and, second, your relationship with money.

The reality is that we all need money to survive, thrive, and have a quality life. Money impacts every area of your daily existence and affects the decisions you make in all areas, particularly in your business or career. If you are a business owner or are self-employed, money and profits are crucial because without them, you cease to exist as a viable enterprise. You miss the opportunity to share your talents, reach and help many people, and create a positive ripple effect.

As such, taking action to transform your relationship with money is critical. It is the first step in achieving wealth and prosperity as well as in tapping into your innermost dreams and desires.

While the focus of this book is on women, I believe that men can also find value in reading it. I wrote this book primarily with women in mind for two key reasons. The first is that as a society we have a tremendous opportunity to benefit from advancing the full participation of women. In fact, women's economic empowerment is vital to achieving a global sustainable future. According to a 2015 McKinsey report, advancing women's equality by narrowing the gender gap in the world of work can add $12 trillion to global economic growth by 2025. In the United States, this figure could add up to

$4.3 trillion in growth if women were to attain full gender equality. This also translates into an extra £150 billion for the United Kingdom. For Canada, a PwC Women in Work 2016 Index report indicates that closing the wage gap and engaging more women in the workforce could lead to $92 billion in GDP.

A by-product of advancing women's global economic empowerment is the generation of greater peace and harmony in the world and of greater healing for our planet. At the Vancouver Peace Summit in 2009, while surrounded by a panel of Nobel Peace Prize laureates, spiritual leaders, world leaders, and dignitaries, His Holiness the Dalai Lama (a Nobel laureate himself) delivered an affecting statement noting, "Some people may call me a feminist.... But we need more effort to promote basic human values — human compassion, human affection. And in that respect, females have more sensitivity for others' pain and suffering." Yet women cannot realize these vast opportunities without the support, cooperation, and collaboration of men, who can play an important role as allies and champions.

The second reason I wrote this book with women in mind is that in order for women to truly seize this tremendous opportunity to stand in their power and own their worth, they must first develop a harmonious relationship with money. Only then can they more effectively benefit from financial literacy — developing the knowledge, skills, and ability to make sound financial decisions to achieve financial well-being. This includes possessing the understanding and skills to manage, save, spend, and donate money as a productive resource.

This book does not focus on the mechanics of financial management, budgeting, saving, and investing. Many great resources for women, related to personal financial planning, management, and investing, are available. Rather, the focus of this book is on helping you understand your beliefs and attitudes about money, achieve a harmonious relationship with money, and develop a deep sense of abundance, thereby creating enduring wealth from within.

You may have been drawn to this book because you want to create more wealth. You may want to become financially independent and have more freedom. Perhaps you want to discover the principles of manifesting wealth and abundance in all areas of your life. You may want to resolve conflicting beliefs and emotions about money so you can create positive beliefs and feel more empowered about money. Or you may want to increase your corporate income. Perhaps you are in transition from the corporate world to the entrepreneurial world and want to more confidently charge what you are worth. As an entrepreneur, you may want more sales, more clients, or a higher income. You may also want to realize your financial dreams and leverage your business and wealth to achieve a much bigger vision and mission in order to make a difference.

Whatever the reasons, you have invited this book into your life because you are on an accelerated path to personal and spiritual growth. This path will enable you to make a positive contribution to the world and to uplift humanity through your life's work.

There has never been a better time for women to take control of our financial independence. In fact, a powerful global shift is taking place in support of women's empowerment. *Now is the best time to serve the world in a bigger way by stepping into your role as the CEO and leader of your life and business, with no apologies.*

The following statistics, collected at the time of this writing, provide a brief snapshot of women's growing economic power:

- Women control $39.6 trillion, approximately 30 percent, of the world's wealth. By 2020 it is estimated that women will control $72.1 trillion of global wealth due to inheritances, settlements, and entrepreneurship.
- There are 190 female billionaires worldwide.
- Women control more than 60 percent of all personal wealth in the United States.
- In higher education, 57 percent of women in the United States hold bachelor's degrees, 60 percent hold master's degrees, and 51 percent hold doctoral degrees.
- In the United States 40 percent of women are the primary or sole breadwinners.
- In the United States 70 percent of women with

children under the age of eighteen participate in the labor force.

- The global incomes of women are predicted to reach $18 trillion by 2018. Women will control close to 75 percent of discretionary spending around the world.
- Women control 85 percent of all purchasing decisions in the United States.

In terms of business, in 2012 the Global Entrepreneurship Monitor estimated that 126 million women were starting or running new businesses in sixty-seven world economies. In addition, an estimated 98 million women were running established businesses (for three years or more). In Canada 15 percent of small to medium businesses are owned by women.

Forbes magazine refers to entrepreneurship as the new "Women's Movement." Since 2007 there has been a rise in women-owned businesses in the Unites States, with 1,072 (net) new women-owned firms launched each day. Between 2007 and 2016 women-owned firms increased by 45 percent, five times the national average. Many women are leaving their corporate jobs to experience greater freedom and flexibility, to find a more meaningful way to make a difference, and to take control of their income and livelihoods.

According to a 2016 State of Women-Owned Businesses Report, commissioned by American Express OPEN, there are 11.3 million women-owned businesses in the

United States, employing close to 9 million people and generating more than $1.6 trillion in revenues.

These figures will continue to grow, owing to a partnership between the governments of Canada and the United States, resulting in the creation of a joint Council for Advancement of Women Entrepreneurs and Business Leaders. The purpose of the initiative is to support women's economic growth by helping to remove barriers to competitiveness for women entrepreneurs as well as to address issues facing women in the workforce, including those faced by senior leaders. This means that women entrepreneurs will have greater access to networks, capital, and markets in starting and growing successful businesses.

There is much to celebrate with these positive advancements. At the same time, there is also much room for improvement. Despite women comprising half the world's population, and representing the largest growing market, they still remain an untapped power. This is particularly the case in four key areas: earnings, leadership, politics, and business income.

In the area of earnings, the wage gap continues to exist:

- On a global average, women earn 77 cents for every dollar men earn.
- In Canada women earn 87 cents for every dollar men earn.

- In the United Kingdom women earn 9.4 percent less than men.
- In the United States women earn 79 cents for every dollar men earn.

In the area of leadership, a 2017 report by Fortune Knowledge Group, in collaboration with Royal Bank of Canada, states that only 4.2 percent of women hold CEO positions in Fortune 500 companies and 9 percent globally.

The reality of these figures contradicts years of research indicating that companies that are engaged in gender diversity and that have women in leadership roles are 15 percent more likely to experience higher financial performance. In the same report, more than 7,500 senior management positions in Fortune 500 companies were identified in 2016, of which 19 percent were held by women.

On corporate boards:

- Globally women held 14.7 percent of board seats in 2015. Only 20 percent of boards have at least three women.
- European countries such as Norway (46.7 percent), France (34 percent), and Sweden (33.6 percent) are leading the way in having the highest percentage of women on their boards.
- Countries with the lowest percentage of women on boards include Taiwan (4.5 percent), South Korea (4.1 percent), and Japan (3.5 percent).

- The percentage of women on corporate boards in the United States is 19.9 percent and 21.6 percent in Canada.
- While the percentages are higher in Europe, women in general are far less likely to lead boards or board committees.
- In the political sphere, as of 2016, globally only one in five people elected to office were women.
- In early 2017 there were ten women serving as heads of state and nine as heads of government around the world.
- In the United States 19 percent of the House of Representatives and 21 percent of the Senate members are women.
- In Canada 26 percent of the House of Commons and 43 percent of the Senate members are women.
- In the United Kingdom 29 percent of the members of Parliament and 26 percent of members in the House of Lords are women.

In the area of entrepreneurship, globally women continue to face various challenges to their success, including limited access to funding, lack of available mentors and role models, an imbalanced share of family work, and a lack of self-confidence. In fact, according to the Kauffman Foundation, nearly 80 percent of women in the tech industry in the United States use personal savings for capital because of limited access.

While the number of female-owned businesses in the United States is growing five times faster than the national average, these businesses are contributing only 4 percent of the nation's business revenues — a share that has not changed during the past twenty years. And despite generating $1.6 trillion in revenues in 2016, 7.9 percent of women generated between $100,000 and $500,000, while only 3.3 percent of women-owned businesses generated more than $500,000 in revenues.

What Holds Women Back?

This brief snapshot provides an opportunity to get to the root of what holds women back. Working with my clients, I have identified several reasons that women may not be doing as well as they could be. For one, often their self-confidence does not match their skill level. Despite their talents, accomplishments, and expertise, many women still question whether they are truly good enough, smart enough, and worthy enough to succeed and prosper financially.

In fact, I have witnessed that regardless of age, educational background, and income level, many women privately struggle with valuing themselves and their worth. This in turn can impact their ability to succeed or grow their business or advance in their career. As Sheryl Sandberg has so famously claimed, women hesitate to "lean in." I have witnessed that women experience a disconnection between:

- what they've accomplished and their level of self-confidence.
- what they really want and what they settle for.
- valuing what they do and valuing their self-worth.
- the determination they show on the outside and the fear and doubt they feel about themselves on the inside.

In my work I encounter many accomplished, talented, and motivated women who are visionary change makers. They want to make a significant contribution to the world and be richly rewarded for the value they provide through their life's work. Deep inside, these ambitious and goal-oriented women want to make a sizable income, make a large impact, and achieve outstanding success. This is inspiring and admirable.

However, what many women actually experience is the opposite. Thus, high-achieving women at various income levels and stages in their business or career seek my help because they want to develop money mastery to achieve success and fulfillment on their own terms. They want to own their fullest worth and express their brilliance. They also want income growth. They are frustrated with their earnings when they do not match the bigger vision they have of their potential. Their income also does not allow them to fund their dreams and social mission or the legacy they want to leave behind.

Some of the challenges these women face include:

- struggling to break through to the next level of income and success.
- feeling anxious about not being able to achieve and exceed their past success, revenue, or salary.
- finding that no matter how hard they work, they are stuck with the same income.

These challenges have puzzled and fascinated me. What was holding these otherwise successful women back from making a meaningful difference doing what they love? Through my training and experience in the area of women and money, as well as my personal journey, I finally realized what the root cause of this issue is. *What holds many women back from making the kind of income they desire and deserve has little to do with their intelligence, motivation, or spirit — but much to do with their relationship to money.*

This was the missing piece of the puzzle. I realized that somehow these women were giving away their personal power through money. This included engaging in self-sabotaging actions that led them to experience money-related stress and anxiety, which impacted their results.

Perhaps what I've described resonates with you. At some point you may have experienced financial challenges or engaged in similar disempowering actions with money.

If so, one way to address these challenges is by

connecting money to your emotions. The most profound and lasting solutions to the challenges you face can be discovered by looking within. I have found that keeping a journal enables me to do so. I also ask my clients to regularly chronicle their emotions and experiences in a journal, which often produces clarity and insights. Writing makes it easier to notice the external obstacles that surface from the deeper emotions of fear and doubt, since they will show up as lack of income, failure to progress, and lack of opportunity. However, it is vital to understand that these external obstacles are simply symptoms of what is really "running the show" — your unconscious feelings and emotions regarding money. These symptoms form the basis of your internal obstacles and emotional blocks to money and wealth.

Since emotions come from within, they are generally harder to recognize on the outside, and harder to overcome. Therefore, these internal obstacles and emotional blocks can keep you from having what you really want and enjoying it once you attain it. In truth, your thoughts and feelings about money are critical factors in determining how much you will make and keep in your life. In other words, your emotional state will ultimately determine your financial state.

Why I Wrote This Book

So why focus on women and their relationship with money? I focus on women and money because it is the fastest way to get to the core of why women hold themselves back. Money is simply a tool to help us uncover something deeper — an opportunity for a breakthrough and transformation in all areas of life.

To put it simply, money is emotional currency for women. Money is tied to our sense of self-worth and self-confidence, and our feelings of safety and security. These emotions can often turn into self-limiting decisions. And the effect can be profound, in terms of either moving you forward or keeping you stuck.

We are all faced with many decisions every day, and those decisions are likely impacted by money. Since you deal with money daily, you can clearly see that your relationship with money plays a decisive role in your success. In fact, your intimate, ongoing relationship with money determines whether you will prosper or struggle in your work and the rest of life. If your relationship with money is left unexamined, you can stay stuck, experiencing a cycle of money drama that acts as a barrier to realizing your full potential and your purpose in life.

My own journey with money has taken me from being a young single mother living from paycheck to paycheck to becoming an award-winning corporate executive and a successful global entrepreneur. I share the details of my own journey with money to let you know that whatever your past or current challenges with money are, they do not define who you are or control your future. You are in charge of your destiny. You can make powerful choices at this moment to create the life you desire.

At a deep soul level this book is really about a rite of passage — an awakening for women to take action to reclaim their feminine connection to money as a source of empowerment, love, wealth, fulfillment, and success. The phrase *feminine connection to money* points to an understanding that there is a natural connection between women, generosity, and leveraging money to help others. And when women reclaim and embrace their feminine connection to money, the results can be remarkable. *When women are empowered with money, they become "difference makers." They create better lives for themselves and their families, give back, contribute to the economy, change the world, and transform lives.*

Therefore, the sooner you empower your relationship with money, the sooner you can take bold actions to claim your wealth and be a force for good. You have a unique mission to fulfill in this lifetime. That mission is to make a difference in your unique way. This may include changing the lives of others for the better. You are meant to fill a place that only you can fill.

You are meant to make an impact that only you can bring about.

Perhaps you are like me and did not start out with the intention of becoming an entrepreneur. Maybe you have experienced a high level of success in the corporate arena or in another industry yet have felt a constant inner restlessness and calling to do, be, and have more. If this is the case, then you are a visionary change maker and you must not settle for less. You want to make a significant impact and be richly rewarded for doing what you love. *There is nothing wrong with wanting or asking for more.*

How to Use This Book

This book is a guide to creating holistic wealth, prosperity, and abundance. It is infused with my lived experience and that of my clients. I discovered many of the concepts presented in this book more than twenty-five years ago and began consciously applying them, making adjustments, and deepening my own learning. My life has been enriched and blessed with greater ease and abundance than I ever could have imagined. Teachers, teachings, resources, and mentors have appeared at pivotal moments to help me advance to the next phase of my life's purpose and journey. I then began teaching these elements to my clients, who were able to achieve great results in their own lives. Now it brings me great joy to share these ideas with you so that you too can align your life's work with your purpose, achieve your fullest potential, and realize your financial goals and dreams.

I invite you to keep an open mind and heart as you embark on this profound inner journey of self-discovery. This journey will help you uncover the nature of your unique relationship with money and ultimately your relationship with yourself. It will also help you to unlock your riches and to recognize that the keys to abundance have always been within you.

You will learn many strategies and tools (in some

cases for the first time) that you can use for years to come in all areas of your life. This includes strategies to manifest what you desire into physical reality. We will take a deeper dive into creating wealth and prosperity using the Eight Holistic Principles of my Wealth Creation System.

In chapters where there is a "Take Action" section following the chapter summary, be sure to download the bonus materials and complete the recommended exercises. Some of the exercises are included in the book and some can be found online, often in greater depth. Then take some time to integrate the insights, learnings, and breakthroughs.

You will read stories of generous, talented women and their relationships with money. For reasons of privacy and confidentiality, the stories are a compilation of client histories and experiences, and I have used fictitious names. I included these anecdotes because they are relatable and inspirational. More important, these accounts can help you recognize the power you gain when you transform your relationship with money and reap the rewards of true happiness, wealth, and abundance.

But this book does much more than help you become empowered financially; it will also inspire you to fulfill your social promise in the world, thereby making it a much better place for all of us.

I believe in you.... Now let's get started!

Part 1

FOUNDATIONS

Chapter 1

SETTING YOURSELF UP
FOR SUCCESS

Begin with the end in mind.
— STEPHEN R. COVEY

BECOMING SUCCESSFUL TAKES COURAGE, passion, ambition, and persistence. Being successful is a personal choice. While the meaning or measure of personal success differs for everyone, some essential elements comprise the success equation. One of these is to set yourself up for success right from the beginning. This includes building a strong foundation for your relationship with money and understanding the deeper meaning that money holds for you. Doing so will accelerate your journey toward realizing your dreams.

Imagine the Possibilities

It is truly rewarding for me to help my clients create harmonious relationships with money. In the initial phase of our work together, I help to place them on the path toward developing money mastery. Once they have overcome and healed any limiting beliefs and emotional blocks about money, we then focus on the second phase of creating wealth through their life's work, as well as creating their ideal lifestyle. This process also includes identifying the social impact they want to make through their life's work. The third and final phase is helping them to fulfill their social promise and to create a positive social impact on the world (see the diagram below).

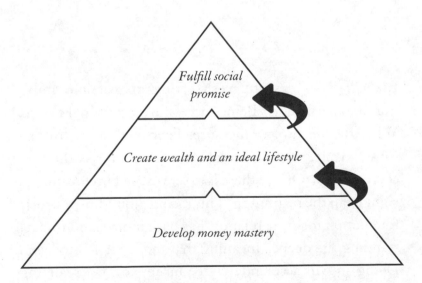

I have witnessed repeatedly that when my clients release their limiting beliefs, emotional blocks, and self-sabotaging actions regarding money, they become unstoppable. They can achieve the financial prosperity they desire while doing what they love and making a positive impact on society. Though this book focuses primarily on the first phase, that of creating a harmonious and abundant relationship with money, we will be touching on the next two phases as well.

Timeless Truths

To gain a deeper understanding of the meaning of money, we need to move beyond the dictionary definition of it as "a measure of value or a means of payment." This deeper comprehension will give you a new perspective on money, which will help you pave the way toward your desired reality. In my work over the past twenty years, I have discovered some essential truths about money, both for myself and for my clients.

The first essential truth is that *money is a uniquely human creation*; it does not exist in nature or in the animal kingdom. The first form of money was used as early as 3000 BCE. And from that time on, humankind has conferred value and power on money. Yet money as an object has no value. It may as well be the artificial currency we use when we play *Monopoly*. The meaning we assign to money is what gives it such prominence, power, and emotional value in our lives. Money has become its own force.

The second essential truth is that *money is an exchange of energy*. We expend energy through our work in exchange for money, another form of energy. In turn, the money enables us to use it in various ways, from acquiring the basic necessities of life to enhancing the quality of our lives and the lives of others. We can also use money to facilitate achieving our goals and dreams.

The third essential truth is that *money is a form of love*. The most powerful force in the Universe is love. It magnifies all the positive qualities of life, such as kindness, faith, hope, generosity, joy, well-being, patience, forgiveness, compassion, peace, courage, happiness, friendship, and more. Therefore, connecting money with love opens up tremendous possibilities for joy because *you* are the source of all your prosperity and wealth.

Money is a tool you can use to take care of yourself and others by showing your love, nurturing, and appreciation. As women, we feel gratified when we can share what we have and help those in need. A tremendous positive domino effect occurs when women are empowered with money. They can help their families and communities while contributing to the economy at the same time. Having said that, it is also essential that as women we give in a way that is balanced, so that we avoid over-giving and sacrificing ourselves.

You can also use money to care for yourself and demonstrate self-love. A key way to do this is to maintain the mind-set that prosperity begins with you. Feeling good about yourself and what you have in your life is

use it to help you fully express yourself through your life's work, and to realize your full potential and higher purpose. Since you have a big mission, money is the tool that will help you accomplish your important work in the world — including transforming lives.

CHAPTER SUMMARY

- To achieve success, you must first build a strong foundation for your relationship with money. Doing so will accelerate your journey to success.
- Money is a uniquely human creation, and as a society we have infused it with a powerful force of its own.
- We expend energy through our work in exchange for money, another form of energy.
- Connecting money with love opens up tremendous possibilities for joy. Money can be used to demonstrate your love, nurturing, and appreciation.
- A tremendous positive ripple effect occurs when women are empowered. You can take care of yourself and your family, help your community, and contribute to the economy and to the world.
- Mastering money and abundance is a powerful journey of personal growth. You can become the best and highest version of yourself in the process.
- You can be rich and spiritual at the same time. There is no need to choose.

- It is not more spiritual or nobler to be poor, for money is often required to accomplish your life's work.
- Let your prosperity reflect the good you contribute to the world. You can use money as a positive and powerful force in service to others and to the world.

Chapter 2

MY MONEY JOURNEY
AND LESSONS

*Our deepest fear is not that we are inadequate. Our deepest fear
is that we are powerful beyond measure. It is our light,
not our darkness, that most frightens us....As we are liberated
from our own fear, our presence automatically liberates others.*
— MARIANNE WILLIAMSON

I WAS BORN IN THE PHILIPPINES, the fourth female and
last child, with three sisters ahead of me. At the time
of my birth, my family was not rich, but neither were
they poor. In fact, I come from a large extended family
of professionals — attorneys, judges, engineers, teachers,
politicians, nurses, accountants, architects, and so on. Yet
the simple fact is I was born in a developing nation with
limited opportunities.

Even as I put these thoughts onto paper, I wonder
what my life would have been like had my parents not
accepted my beloved aunt's invitation to immigrate to
Canada when I was four. That one act of kindness, and

my parents' calculated decision to uproot their young family and leave behind all that they knew to begin a new life halfway across the world, was courageous and admirable. More important, that one act of compassion profoundly changed the trajectory and quality of my life forever. I am eternally grateful to my aunt and my parents.

Although I do not remember the journey itself, I do know that my parents' decision spared me from witnessing the daily realities of the extreme disparities in wealth that exist between the rich and poor in my birth country. It also saved me from experiencing the frustration of having untapped potential and unrealized dreams. Instead, growing up in a prosperous country paved the way for my many opportunities and successes.

Fortunately, my parents were both college graduates and able to quickly build a solid foundation in their adopted land. I marvel at the fact that my mother earned a bachelor of commerce degree back in 1958, when women around the globe — especially in a developing nation — were not widely engaged in higher education. From when I was a young child until she reached retirement age, my mother had a corporate career, and I believe her fierce determination had a huge impact on me.

Since I was seven years old I have been fascinated with money, wealth, and success and captivated by the people who have it. Questions such as "How did they become wealthy and successful?" and "What is the secret to a life of wealth and abundance?" were ones I often pondered early on. As I grew older, I became curious as to why

some people were able to create wealth from humble beginnings, while others who had wealth could manage to
lose it all. This fascination with prosperity stayed with
me throughout adolescence and into adulthood. It was
not a daily thought but something that was frequently,
if quietly, in the background of my consciousness. It was
only much later that I finally realized the real purpose of
this fascination.

My career choice at the age of twelve was to be a journalist, particularly to do what Barbara Walters did —
interviewing people, learning about them, and sharing
their inspiring stories. I loved what Walters did; she was
a true trailblazer who paved the way for many women
in her industry. Years later, I discovered Oprah Winfrey
and admired her inspirational way of uplifting people to
realize their fullest potential and higher calling and to
follow their dreams. Her generosity and philanthropic
spirit are beautiful expressions of social promise in action.

Yet, though my parents did relatively well for themselves, one characteristic they were unable to easily overcome was their mind-set regarding money, and this
mind-set affected me as well. They inherited generations
of cultural beliefs and values regarding money, which
primarily focused on fear, doubt, and lack. They were
both very young children during World War II, when
they endured hardships and were forced to go without
many of life's comforts.

I recall early on making a conscious choice to move
beyond this outlook. Even at that young age, I knew there

was so much more that I was meant to do, be, and have. I simply knew that I was not on this earth to play small, since I had a bigger purpose — although I could not have imagined what it was at that time. By the time I was fifteen I was ready to adopt a different view of money, one that was more positive and productive. I had a part-time job, which gave me some independence and some experience with managing money. But it wasn't till years later that I fully realized that I had the power to release my family's legacy regarding money, adopt a new mind-set, and create different results in my life.

Blessings in Disguise

While I was at university, like many young people, I went through a rebellious phase, which again changed the course of my life path. My studies were interrupted by big life events, and by the age of twenty-three I had undergone what it takes many women years or even decades to experience. I was married briefly, became a mother, got divorced, and was living on my own with my precious baby daughter. It all happened in a flash.

I had very quickly realized that I was living the wrong life with the wrong partner. During that time, I gave my financial power away while staying home to take care of my baby. I had to rely on my partner for money, which did not sit well with me. Within six months, I decided to leave the relationship, knowing that my and my daughter's future would have been bleak had I stayed. Although my parents were generous in offering us a place in their home, I wanted to be on my own and craved freedom and independence.

Living on my own with a small baby in a large city was not easy. In fact, it was scary at times. I had a sheltered upbringing and did not know how to be on my own. I didn't even know how to cook, so I had to learn fast. At this point I decided not to apply for social assistance. It was available to me, but I was determined to make it on my own. I also decided not to pursue child support. While not ideal, at the time I was only too happy to forgo these things so that I could quickly move on and secure my independence.

Getting a well-paying job was at the top of my list. Fortunately, I got a job in a research hospital after just a few weeks of looking. My daughter and I lived in an old but cozy one-bedroom low-rise apartment in an upscale neighborhood with a large park and a beautiful church across the street, which eased my mind.

The only help I accepted was with childcare. I was able to secure a spot for my daughter at a coveted daycare center because, during the government elections, I decided to leverage the campaigns and badgered the mayor's office to take my daughter off the waiting list so that I could keep my job. She was close to last on the list, which meant months of waiting for an opening. Miraculously, the next day she had her spot. That was a defining moment for me as I realized I could manifest my desires by asking for what I wanted. More specifically, I realized that I was a powerful manifester and could achieve anything that I set my mind on. My "aha" moment was that when you are completely aligned with your intention and take action on that alignment, the Universe joins and supports you.

Those were memorable years for me. My entry-level salary was decent, but I was also left with high credit card debt and a student loan. I decided to take full responsibility for my finances, which led me to close my credit card accounts and pay for everything in cash. This meant that if I didn't have the money, I couldn't purchase something. It took me four years to pay off the credit cards and student loan in full; I had such a sense of accomplishment when I completed the payments. It was a good plan because I paid every bill on time, thereby maintaining a good credit rating — no credit card company or collection agency ever called me to demand money owed.

While I did not have much in the way of material possessions or savings, with just enough for rent, food, transportation, and incidentals after the bills, I was happy, optimistic, and hopeful for a much brighter future. An essential lesson I learned about money during this time was the importance of not denying myself some extras from time to time, particularly on special occasions such as birthdays, so that I would not feel like I was in a cycle of lack. This made a big difference in my outlook.

Mind-set is everything because if I had had a different perspective, things could have gone in a much different direction. In those years I never once thought of myself as poor. It did not even enter my thoughts — not because I worked at keeping those ideas away but simply because I never identified with them. This is a key outlook.

My perspective on my relationship with money during that phase was that everything I needed would be provided for, and somehow it always was. It was at this time that I began to make the connection between money and spiritual laws, which we will discuss in full later in the book.

A blessing and a silver lining was meeting my husband. Everything fell into place quickly, just as I had envisioned, including his deep bond with my daughter. Soon thereafter we got married and bought our first house. This gave me the opportunity to go back to school and on to graduate school, where I majored in social policy and management.

A Life of Service and Contribution

The idea of making a contribution, being of service, and making a difference has always mattered to me. It led me to follow in my father's footsteps and focus on the public service arena. My work contributed to many initiatives, including Canada's first-ever legislation for people with disabilities; creating equal-opportunity policies for disadvantaged groups; and helping women achieve financial independence. Over the years, I assumed progressive senior leadership roles with a broader span of influence and large teams, and I was managing and spending eight-figure budgets. My executive career in the public sector was very rewarding.

My relationship with money became harmonious. There was a consistent flow of abundance and blessings, which enabled our family to live comfortably. My daughter was happy and thriving, which is, of course, the greatest blessing for a parent. We enjoyed vacations abroad, a large home, and beautiful things and surroundings. By this time my humble beginnings seemed like they belonged to a distant past.

It seemed like a charmed life. The only issue was that I persistently felt like I was meant to do something more, to be more, and to realize a much broader mission. Although I had all the trappings of success, something was missing. My body was signaling me to get connected with what I needed in order to feel joyful, but I was too busy to pay attention. My days felt like I was in a scene from *The West Wing* television show, with endless crises to solve and meetings to chair. I felt driven to get results, often eating lunch late in the day or not at all, and working late into the night. While making a contribution through public service was a big motivator for me, it began to take its toll.

Life always has a way of making you pay attention, usually in a dramatic way. I experienced a turning point with my health in the form of burnout, induced by stress, which impacted my low-functioning immune system. There were days where I could not get out of bed, despite my best efforts. Simply put, I was depleted physically and emotionally. My quality of life was declining, and I knew that something had to change. This experience was the jolt I needed to reassess what I truly wanted.

This reassessment ultimately led me to walk away from a successful fifteen-year, six-figure career to follow a deeper calling. I had just received my postgraduate designation as a professional certified coach, so I knew the timing was perfect for a new adventure. I quickly decided to hand in my resignation, which shocked many people because I was at the height of my career. But I wanted to start a new and meaningful chapter and begin my entrepreneurial journey, so I took a leap of faith.

An unexpected and wonderful opportunity occurred shortly after I left my career. An invitation arrived to attend a gala event, along with my former team, to receive a prestigious award for our work making a difference in the lives of hundreds of thousands of children, youths, and their families. This award of excellence is given only to a select few, so I cherish it as the perfect ending to my public service career, knowing that I made an impact.

The Call

Life is like a beautiful mosaic in which all the intricate pieces of our experiences fit together to prepare us for the next step of our journey. No one experience is a waste, even if we regard it as minor or insignificant. My years of experience in senior leadership positions granted me firsthand experience of women's empowerment and the importance of realizing financial independence and self-responsibility in regard to money.

When I began working with women as a life coach, I noticed that sooner or later, the conversation always turned to the topic of money. Money was a source of either worry or fear, or both. It seemed to be the key factor that people attributed either to a life well lived or to a life that was difficult and constrained. Somehow we started to equate having money with having permission to live fully and well.

As I began to work with women entrepreneurs, I realized that money is emotional currency for women and is innately connected to their sense of self-confidence and self-worth, and that these emotions are further heightened when these entrepreneurs are generating income in their businesses.

Personally, I believed I had harmonized my own relationship with money long ago. Yet when I became an entrepreneur, it took me back to my childhood and my feelings about money and past experiences that I had forgotten. I had to say, "Oh hello, old friend. You're back." This made me realize that there is always room for more personal growth and that this growth had to start with further healing and harmonizing my relationship with money. I resolved to work with top coaches and mentors, who assisted me in breaking through my mental and emotional blocks and resistance regarding money, helping me to move forward.

This work included releasing and changing my old

money story, related to old habits of overspending, which had kept me stuck, frustrated, and disconnected from manifesting wealth in greater abundance. There was a misalignment between what I believed I deserved and what I truly believed was possible for me to manifest into reality. Once I started to believe that my ability to transform people's lives and create a positive ripple effect was a direct reflection of the prosperity that could also come into my life, everything began to fall into place with greater flow and abundance.

Full Circle

Sensing a great need to help women transform their relationship with money, I began to focus my efforts on learning more about this captivating relationship, receiving certification and training specifically in the area of women and money, as well as creating tools and strategies to help women make breakthroughs from within. I founded my company and combined my twenty-year leadership experience, expertise, and training, as well as my lived experience, into expressing my life's work. Today I am on a mission to empower women to rise and thrive as leaders, as entrepreneurs, and as professionals — living lives of purpose, wealth, and significance while being a force for good in the world. In many ways it feels as if I have come full circle. Am I entirely free of money-related anxieties? Certainly not. Nor are those with vast incomes. Here is an example: In the last season of her

TV show, Oprah Winfrey interviewed J.K. Rowling, author of the bestselling Harry Potter series. She asked Rowling about her feelings regarding money, and her perception of herself now that she is known as the first billionaire author. Rowling noted that the great gift of money is freedom from anxiety, but given her past experiences as a single mother living on government benefits, she will never take it for granted and never completely stop worrying about it. Both Winfrey and Rowling came from humble beginnings, have attained enormous fame, and are self-made billionaires, yet they still think about the security of their wealth.

I believe that nurturing, strengthening, and being at peace with my relationship with money is a lifelong commitment. Some situations still trigger emotions for me; however, I have the mind-set, tools, and strategies in place to help me move forward with greater joy, grace, and ease than ever before. You can have this too. It gives me great pleasure to be able to share my journey with you.

CHAPTER SUMMARY

- Whatever your past or current challenges with money are, they do not define who you are or dictate your future. You are in charge of your destiny. You can make powerful choices to create the prosperous life and future you desire.
- You have the power to let go of your family's history with money.

- You can create your new empowered money story and realize positive results when you start to believe that what you desire is truly possible to achieve.

- You already possess the ability to be a powerful manifester. Whatever you have in your life is something that you manifested — both the good and the not so good.

- When you are aligned with the intention of what you want to achieve and you take inspired actions, the Universe, through experiences, resources, people, and synchronicities of events, will support you.

- Be mindful and purposeful with money in how you earn it, spend it, and keep it. This will enable you to use money not only as a tool for fulfilling your goals but also as a force for good.

- Nurturing and strengthening your relationship with money is a lifelong commitment.

- All your experiences matter, even if you regard some as minor or insignificant.

- Your life is like a beautiful mosaic in which all the intricate pieces of your experiences, expertise, talents, and accomplishments fit perfectly together to prepare you for the next step of your life's journey.

Chapter 3

WOMEN AND MONEY

We are progressing in virtually all other areas of our lives.
Money issues are a kind of a last frontier in our development.
— DR. C. DIANE EALY AND DR. KAY LESH

DID YOU KNOW that the word *money* comes from the name of the Roman goddess Juno Moneta? She guarded the Roman Empire's finances, and a temple overlooking the Roman Forum was built in her honor in 344 BCE. Every time we use the word *money*, we are invoking the goddess's name.

Though the Romans chose a female deity to guard over their finances, as time went on, there was little mention of women's connection to power and money. Instead, for centuries, because of regressive laws, women's financial existence was dependent on men — their fathers, husbands, brothers, uncles, and sons.

This is no longer the case in many countries, especially in the Western world. As already noted, 70 percent of women in the United States with children under the age of eighteen participate in the labor force and contribute to overall family income. Many are actively seeking ways to increase their financial security by purchasing books, going to money management workshops and seminars, seeking help from financial advisors, experts, and so on.

Yet I've learned from my experience in working with women that more knowledge alone will not help you create financial independence and security unless you first examine and improve your overall relationship with money. Do you wonder what shapes your relationship with money, and that of women in general? To help us gain a better understanding of women's relationships with money, I offer a brief review of our history and traditions. While many influences shape women's relationships with money, I will focus on three main areas: family, culture, and society.

What Does Family Have to Do with It?

Your family history and place of origin play a significant role in forming your ideas about money. Taking a look at how money was regarded and handled in your family can have a powerful effect on your relationship with money.

Families use money in many ways: to express love, to reward, to control, to support, to punish, to share, to respect, to fear, to give thanks, to cultivate responsibility or dependency, and much more. Money can also stir up feelings of envy, competition, comparison, a sense of belonging, and power. These experiences shape your feelings about money — whether you trust money or whether it causes anxiety; how you share, accept, and receive money; and how you use money for your own means.

Perhaps you saw your grandmother or mother turn over the household finances to your father, grandfather, or uncles. Perhaps you heard that there was not enough money for college, so the males in the family received a better education than the females. Maybe you have heard your family and relatives arguing over money or the contents of a will.

Or maybe you witnessed the positive, empowering ways that the women in your family dealt with money. Perhaps the women in your family were just as well educated as, or better educated than, the men. Maybe as early as you can remember your mother also had a career and contributed to the family income. This was the case with my own extended family. Everyone — males and females alike — was required to have an education and secure a career or job outside the home. As mentioned earlier, my mother had a career until she reached retirement age, so my sisters and I were expected to attend a university, become professionals, contribute to society, and pave the way for the next generation.

Historically, in most families, the husbands and fathers were the breadwinners who controlled the financial decisions, which placed women in dependent roles. Women's roles traditionally have been identified with nurturing, homemaking, caring for the children, and so forth, plus supporting their husbands with their careers. That is why divorce can adversely affect women's finances, often causing them to experience a dramatic drop in their standard of living and quality of life.

Every family, including yours, has its own money story or legacy, and every generation adds its own. And when emotions are added to the story, it can become legendary. Whatever your family story with money is, these experiences are likely deeply ingrained within you and the cause of some of your internal struggles with money.

LAURA'S STORY

Laura is a happily married writer with two children. When she was growing up, her family had little in the way of material things, and her parents let her brother and sisters know it.

Her parents were not frivolous with money. Laura watched her mother "stretch the dollar" quite effectively. She would go shopping with her mother to buy groceries and clothes for everyone; everything was purchased on sale, never at the regular price.

When we began working together, Laura was having a hard time shopping for clothes. Her husband, Nick, who'd had a different experience with money growing up, was the opposite. Sometimes he even told Laura to lighten up. It was hard for Laura to let go of her money, especially if an item was not on sale.

She described to me an internal battle that took place when she shopped. It took Laura a long time to decide whether to make a purchase. This exhausted her because having the money to pay for the purchases wasn't even the issue — her family's history with funds (or the lack thereof) was.

Our work included helping Laura to heal her emotions of fear and anxiety related to her family's beliefs about money. The root of her internal battle came from not wanting to disrespect her parents, so she continued to uphold their old beliefs, even if they didn't serve her.

The turning point came when Laura forgave her parents and herself for adopting these false beliefs about money, especially since she saw many examples of abundance (not lack) in her own life. Once Laura released these false beliefs, and adopted new and empowered beliefs about money, the internal battle that took place when she spent money while shopping finally ceased.

A Cultural Shift:
The Joy of Financial Independence

Our culture defines the role money plays in our lives and dictates the right behaviors and ethics relating to money. Making good money is valued in our culture as a sign of prestige and status. Today in most Western cultures women are no longer expected to depend on men for their financial security. You are fully responsible for your financial independence and for how you earn, invest, save, and spend your money.

As any advertiser can tell you, a key aspect of our culture of consumerism is devoted to women and shopping. After all, women control 85 percent of all purchasing decisions. In the past, women were financially marginalized and did not have the opportunity to consume. This is no longer the case. Women's shopping behaviors are now glorified by the phrases "shop till you drop" and "born to shop."

How do you feel about shopping? Does it relieve loneliness and boredom by offering distractions? Does it provide a means of interacting with others and the world at large? Does it enhance your self-confidence and image? Does it provide an endorphin high, a form of self-soothing? Or do spending sprees, like various addictive behaviors, produce a remorseful low? The fact is, shopping can be a way to compensate for feeling unappreciated, devalued, or neglected. It can be an expensive way to fill a void in our lives. Driven by these emotions, shoppers can often be driven to compulsively overspend.

While consumerism is widespread in our culture, there is also a shift toward less consumption, in part to help protect the environment and in part due to the recognition that human connections are a more important part of leading a fulfilled life than material things.

JANET'S STORY

Janet admitted that she was a compulsive shopper. She loved to buy luxurious gifts for herself and her loved ones. After all, she was making a good income, so she could indulge herself. Her husband, Joe, disapproved of her spending habits and tried to curtail them.

Janet had a way of hiding her purchases and would tell her husband that the items she purchased were on sale, even if that was not the case. The problem was that her spending was getting out of control. She was simply spending more than she was making — plus, her credit card debt was ballooning.

As we worked together, Janet admitted she was not being honest about money with herself or her husband. She also uncovered the real reason for her compulsive spending. At the core, she was unhappy and experiencing midlife blues. Janet regretted that she had never made time to have children. She also resented working long hours in her business because it was consuming her life and affecting her health and well-being. Janet also took exception to the fact that despite her working overtime, her hard work did not seem to be making any difference because for the past three years she had not been able to break into six figures. This insight was the catalyst that enabled Janet to come to terms with her anger toward herself.

Janet resolved to take three necessary actions to

change her relationship with money. First, she had an honest conversation with her husband about the state of her finances and the root cause of her behavior and sadness. The conversation she most dreaded turned out to be a blessing, bringing her and Joe much closer together. Second, since Janet felt loved and supported, she took another big step to create and follow an action plan to pay off her debts and curb her spending.

The third action, and perhaps the most critical one, was that Janet shifted her view of her finances, seeing them not as a source of shame but as a tool for personal growth. This shift freed up her energy to focus positively on her work. She began to love her business again, which put her on the path to breaking into the six-figure mark within ten months — much sooner than she had anticipated.

Reforming Societal Messages

Our conditioning as women regarding money is also formed by the messages we receive from our patriarchal society, the media, advertising, and even fairy tales. Think about stories such as "Cinderella," "Sleeping Beauty," "Snow White," and "Rapunzel," which have repeatedly been used as a formula in novels and Hollywood romantic movies. These folk tales' basic premise is that somewhere out there is a prince who will one day come to take the maiden away from all her troubles, bestowing the riches, love, and security that have been missing from her life. The message is that these women can rely on certain attributes — beauty, charm, and kind hearts — to find their Prince Charming but not on their intelligence, ambition, and talents. For generations, these messages have served to ingrain in girls the belief that they are not capable of earning their own living and of managing money.

On some unconscious (or maybe not so unconscious) level, many women have identified with the message that someone will come and rescue them from having to learn how to take care of themselves and their finances. This leaves women vulnerable and disempowered. This patriarchal message plays on women's psyches, especially since feeling safe is very important to girls and women. In fact, separating money and security is difficult, since they are bound together in women's minds. For women this can lead to staying in relationships that are not good or healthy for them, as they trade their freedom for the sense of safety. Women may put up with their partner's infidelity or drinking problem or even abusive treatment for the sake of perceived security.

The "money = security" message came from a time when women who were married were more secure than those who were single. This idea can also spill over into our businesses and careers, causing women to stay in unhealthy work situations for the same reason — wanting to have security. Of course, true security comes from knowing who you are and what is most important to you. Inner security is your true source of strength.

JASMINE'S STORY

Jasmine left a lucrative career in sales to work from home as a consultant. This gave her the flexibility to be with her three-year-old son, Ben, who has special needs. Although she was earning a good income on her own, with her son's health issues, Jasmine had been afraid to leave her unhappy marriage out of fear that being on her own would jeopardize her quality of life and that of her son.

When Jasmine was growing up, her mother would say security came from having a husband. So Jasmine bought into this message and was willing to forgo her own happiness in exchange for having security. She felt stuck.

As we began to dig deeper, Jasmine acknowledged that her need for security was a "sneaky" fear from her childhood conditioning and that the best course of action was to face her fear directly. The first step involved having a courageous conversation with her husband. During that emotional conversation, they both admitted that their marriage was no longer a source of happiness, especially since most of their energy was consumed by arguments brought on by the stress of worrying about their son's health. While doing so was scary, they both agreed to separate.

Emboldened by her action, Jasmine's next courageous

conversation was with her mother. Her goal was to be honest about everything and not seek approval. To her surprise, her mother was very supportive of her decision, and even offered to help.

For the first time since Ben was born, Jasmine had a great night of sleep, finally releasing all her emotional baggage and feeling free and relieved. She confronted her fears and didn't fall apart. Then Jasmine decided to give herself permission to think bigger about her life and her work. Over time, Jasmine hired expert help for Ben, which benefited her and her family. She also began to thrive personally and professionally — succeeding on her own terms.

How Women Perceive Money

In the book *The Female Brain*, neuropsychiatrist Dr. Louann Brizendine describes the differences between women's and men's brains in terms of structure and functionality. The female brain, for example, has considerably more connecting brain cells than the male brain. This means that women can hold more information at once and have a greater ability to multitask. Men's brains, on the other hand, are wired to focus on one task at a time. Women's brains are also more amenable to change and thinking about things from different perspectives to incorporate more information. For males, the emphasis is on linear thinking, facts, and figures.

Another interesting aspect regarding the female brain is that women have a larger capacity for emotion, language, communication, and memory. On average, women are better at expressing emotions, forming connections, being emotionally sensitive, and remembering details. Women's thoughts and speech are informed by a sense of empathy, cues to body language, and intuition. In fact, according to Brizendine, during the first three months of life, a baby girl's skills in making eye contact and mutual facial gazing will increase at a rate of over 400 percent, whereas facial gazing skills in a baby boy will not increase at all.

Baby girls are born already interested in emotional expressions. They take meaning about themselves from a look, a touch, and every reaction they receive from the people they interact with. Based on the cues they receive, baby girls begin to discover their sense of self and whether they are worthy, lovable, or bothersome.

So what does this have to do with money? Since they have more connecting brain cells than men, women do not see money in isolation. Rather, we see it as a part of a web of relationships. This means that you are more likely to take your strong feelings for others, as well as your relationships, into consideration when making money-related decisions. You are also likely to take into consideration how you can share what you have with others who are less fortunate.

For women, the motivation to have money is about relationships and how we can use money to express love

— by taking care of ourselves or our loved ones, or giving money away to help others. This is a distinctive quality of the feminine connection to money.

For men, however, money often signifies power and position and can play out in scenes of competition and accumulation. Men may use money to establish their stature in society and to assert their masculinity and power, as reflected in business-page stories about deals, acquisitions, and mergers of companies. From my personal experience and my work with other women, I would say that the difference between women and men in regards to money can be summed up this way: *men ask for what they want, while women ask for what they think they deserve.*

Women have tried to conform to capitalism's norms by adopting more masculine behaviors with money, behaviors that exemplify individualism, aggressiveness, and power. An example of this kind of behavior is the emphasis on profits alone as the primary measure of success, often at the expense of employees and their well-being. In the process, the feminine values of interdependence, connections, and caring have become less recognized.

The truth is that in regards to money, and indeed all other things, a balance of both the feminine and masculine is needed, since there are also some challenges with adopting solely feminine energy. For example, women's desire for inclusiveness can lead to problems with setting boundaries and having appropriate limits. But never fear. The steps put forth in this book will help you develop a more harmonious and balanced relationship with money and with yourself.

A Turning Point

We are at a pivotal juncture in our history where there is heightened awareness and support of women's empowerment, particularly with advancing women's economic empowerment. I believe that each of us must be awake to our good. We must be ready to seize the opportunity when presented.

On an individual level, we can take action to fully stand in our power and own our worth. Women can also collectively seize the moment and leverage this wave of support to make significant contributions to creating a global sustainable future. And the key way to do so is to embrace our feminine connection to money.

Embodying the feminine connection to money can include the following:

- Embracing the natural connection between women, generosity, and using money as an expression of love and a way to help others
- Recognizing and promoting the potential of money to create a ripple effect to uplift humanity and the planet
- Nurturing the connection of money to love, compassion, meaning, and cooperation, which can lead to personal and collective empowerment — a win-win for all

- Leveraging money as a powerful force for good — generating greater peace, harmony, and healing in the world

By embracing the feminine connection to money as a source of strength, we can simultaneously equate women with wealth, empowerment, and success.

CHAPTER SUMMARY

- Your family's history, attitudes, and behaviors regarding money have an effect on your relationship with money.
- Culture, society, and the media have also helped shape your relationship with money.
- You are fully responsible for your financial independence and for how you earn, invest, save, and spend your money.
- Women do not see money in isolation. Rather, we see it as a part of a web of relationships.
- You are likely to consider how you can share your money and possessions with others who are less fortunate. This instinct comes naturally to women, who want to give back and make a meaningful difference.
- Feeling safe is very important to women, who tend to equate money with security.
- Having true security, however, comes from knowing who you are as well as knowing what is most important to you. Inner security is your true source

of strength, knowing that you — and you alone — are the master of your destiny.

- Now is the time to reclaim and embrace your feminine connection to money as a source of strength and empowerment.

Part 2

DEVELOPING MASTERY

Chapter 4

DISCOVERING YOUR
FINANCIAL STARTING POINT

*Find the courage to break those agreements that are fear-based
and claim your personal power.*
— DON MIGUEL RUIZ

Now THAT WE HAVE DISCUSSED the benefits of advancing
women's economic empowerment, examined the context
for building a strong foundation with money, and discovered the deeper meaning that money holds for women,
we are ready to embark on a journey — an inner journey
to unlock your prospects for financial prosperity that will
change your relationship with yourself and your money.
The journey is one of getting on, and staying on, the path
to a prosperous future. If you want to be well equipped
for the journey ahead, be sure to keep the following nine
tips in mind:

1. **Give yourself permission.** As women we look for approval and permission. I invite you *not* to wait for anyone else to give you permission. Give *yourself* permission. Keep an open mind and heart. That includes being grateful for who you are right now (warts and all), for arriving at this moment, and for being open to all that is about to unfold.

2. **Be honest.** Remember that you are the only one who will see your responses to the exercises included in the book and online unless you decide to share them with others. To really get to the root of your feelings, beliefs, and attitudes regarding money, you need to be as honest as you can with yourself. We all keep secrets from ourselves about our true feelings, especially when it comes to money.

3. **Put yourself first.** Commit to taking care of yourself and putting your needs at the top of the priority list, which is a way to practice being "self-fulfilled" rather than "selfish." Ultimately it is about loving yourself. When you do, you will experience positive changes, and so will those around you because you are operating at your best. Putting yourself first can include scheduling uninterrupted "alone time" for reflection as you read and complete the exercises in this book. It can also include time for meditation, being still, and getting in touch with your emotions.

4. **Start a money gratitude journal.** Choose a journal that feels just right for you, preferably one with lots of room for writing. (Or open a brand-new file on

your computer, and use some nice graphics to make it special.) A journal will serve as a safe space for self-reflection. You may already be familiar with journaling and already have a gratitude journal (a diary about things and people you are grateful for that accentuates the positive). In this case you will be taking gratitude journaling a step further by focusing on what you are grateful for related to money. What you focus on grows, so focus on being thankful for your money, and you will start to see positive changes.

5. **Forgive.** Forgive yourself, and forgive others who have helped frame your relationship with money. A key way to move beyond your emotional obstacles with money is to let them go and to forgive whoever was involved with setting those hurdles in your way. This action can be very powerful, since forgiveness is likely what stands between you and having more money and abundance in your life.

6. **Feel prosperous now.** No matter how much you have or don't have, no matter what your income is at this moment, begin and continue to feel prosperous right now. It is essential not to label yourself as poor because that brings your energy and thoughts toward poverty consciousness, which is definitely *not* your goal.

7. **Pay attention to synchronicities.** As you begin to transform your relationship with money, you will send energy out to the Universe regarding your intention. Pay attention to coincidences, synchronicities, and opportunities that come your way. These could

occur in the form of meeting new contacts, clients, or colleagues at unexpected locations; hearing about a mentor, book, or program that may move you forward; or just being in the right place at the right time.

8. **Celebrate the big and the small.** We tend to acknowledge only the big achievements and not the smaller steps that we took to get there. They all count, so be sure to celebrate the baby steps on your way to reaping the big rewards.

9. **Have fun!** You are on an adventure of self-discovery, love, courage, and possibility, so play, laugh, be imaginative, express your true heart's desire and creativity, and manifest your dreams!

Ready...Set...Go!

Keeping these tips in mind, it's time to get real and identify your financial starting point — a baseline of your current relationship with money, which you can track while progressing on this transformative inner journey. You will uncover insights that will surprise you. This process provides a wonderful opportunity to look at your fears around money and to overcome them. I have come to believe that all the advice in the world regarding money is ineffective unless we first overcome the mental and emotional blocks that are holding us back from wealth, abundance, and success. The following strategies and exercises build on discussions in previous chapters, and provide insights into your specific situation.

Here are two strategies to get you started. The first is to take stock of your current relationship with money. In your journal, write your answers to the following five questions:

1. What is your current relationship with money?
2. How do you feel about money, and why?
3. What is your earliest memory of money?
4. What and who has influenced your view of money?
5. On a scale of 1 to 10 (with 10 being the highest), how satisfied are you with your financial life? Why?

The second strategy is to take stock of how prosperous you are right now, using the Holistic Wealth Wheel exercise below. This useful exercise provides a snapshot of your overall *prosperity*. Keep these three points in mind when completing the exercise. First, the word *prosperity* has a broad meaning in that it includes wealth, affluence, success, profitability, luxury, ease, security, plenty, a state of well-being, and a state of mind.

Next, remember that everything in your life is interconnected; what you do in one area of your life affects another. This also applies to money, since your financial life is reflected in all aspects of your life. In other words, money serves as a *mirror* of all the other facets of your life and often reflects back a specific behavior. Maybe this seems like a stretch, so let me share an example. When a woman lacks self-confidence in asking for a raise or having important money-related conversations with the bank or with her partner, she is likely also lacking self-confidence in asserting herself in her business or career or in her relationships with her partner, family, and friends. Perhaps she is also lacking self-confidence in her parenting ability.

Third, taking a holistic approach to viewing prosperity and wealth includes not just how many dollars you earn or how much you have saved but also your health, love and relationships, family and friends, spirituality, recreation and fun, environment, and life's work.

See the graphic below and the instructions on the next page. At the end of the chapter, you will also find instructions for downloading the exercise.

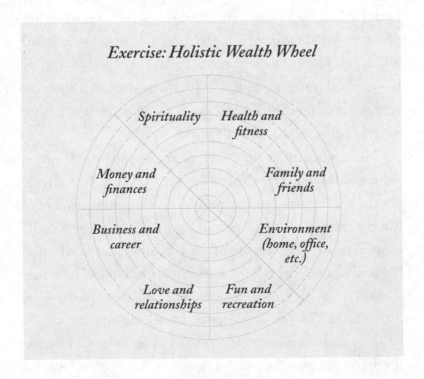

Exercise: Holistic Wealth Wheel

Spirituality

Health and fitness

Money and finances

Family and friends

Business and career

Environment (home, office, etc.)

Love and relationships

Fun and recreation

INSTRUCTIONS: Consider the center of the wheel as 0 and the rings as 1 to 10, with the outer edge as 10. Rank your level of satisfaction in each area from 1 to 10 (with 10 as the highest level of satisfaction). Mark the line of the specific pie area with a dot. Once all the lines are marked, connect the dots. Here is an example of how the "wheel" might look for someone whose highest levels of satisfaction are in the areas of "Fun and recreation," "Environment," and "Spirituality."

Now assess the overall richness of your life. How even is your wheel?

Creating New Truths

By completing the exercises above, you have taken the initial steps to assessing your financial starting point.

What "aha" moment did you have about your relationship with money? This insight is vital to creating your new and more empowered truths regarding money. I know from experience that it takes courage to be financially successful. You are required to face your fears, be honest with yourself, and take action to overcome the fears and doubts that are affecting your relationship with your money and with yourself.

Most of all, creating your new money truths requires you to believe that you can do it — that you can, and are willing to, look within; that you can, and are willing to, face and overcome your inner obstacles; and that you can, and are willing to, uncover your riches.

I applaud you for taking action. I know you can do it!

CHAPTER SUMMARY

- You are on an inner journey to change your relationship with yourself and your money, helping you to unlock your financial prosperity.
- Everything in your life is interconnected; what you do in one area of your life impacts another. This also applies to money, since your financial life is reflected in all the other areas of your life.
- Money can mirror other parts of your life.
- Nine tips to keep in mind on your journey: Give yourself permission; be honest; put yourself first; start your money journal; forgive yourself and others; feel prosperous now; pay attention to

synchronicities; celebrate the small steps along the way to the big achievements; and have fun!

- Two strategies for discovering your financial starting point are taking stock of your current relationship with money, and taking stock of how prosperous you are right now in your life by using the Holistic Wealth Wheel exercise.

- Gaining awareness of your financial starting point is a great opportunity to assess your doubts and fears about money so you can overcome them.

- Creating your new money truths requires you to face your fears and be very honest with yourself as a way to overcome the obstacles that are affecting your relationship with your money, and yourself.

- Most of all, creating your new money truths requires you to believe that you can do it.

Take Action

Bonus download at:
www.MoneyManifestationAndMiracles.com/gift

Holistic Wealth Wheel Exercise

Chapter 5

MANIFESTING FINANCIAL PROSPERITY

*All of creation, everything that exists in the physical world,
is the result of the unmanifest transforming itself into the manifest.*
— DEEPAK CHOPRA

As YOU MOVE FORWARD on your journey toward developing money mastery and creating a harmonious relationship with money, it is vital to understand the concept of manifesting. Essentially, manifesting is about transforming something you deeply desire into physical reality. It is a means of creatively channeling energy into desired ends and goals. Understanding this process will assist you in achieving all your life goals, including your financial ones.

In this chapter, you will discover three vital elements related to manifesting financial prosperity, success, and well-being. The first vital element is the Universal and

Spiritual Laws of financial prosperity and money; the second is the Core Manifesting Process; and the third is the Key Manifesting Tools, in which you apply the first two vital elements. I have seen, from personal experience, that these three vital elements, when combined and used properly, can help you manifest miracles.

From the perspective of manifesting, all creation is a result of intentional thoughts, which when expressed through deliberate actions can manifest your desire. In fact, one could claim that without having clear thoughts about what you wish to achieve, it would be impossible to manifest it.

Ultimately, your thoughts, positive or negative, create your subjective reality — from the intangible to the tangible. At a conscious or unconscious level, your thoughts have invited various experiences into your life, both positive and negative. That is, you will attract into your life whatever you think of most, whatever you strongly believe in, and whatever you expect to occur on a deep level. As an example, when you are consistently fearful or anxious about a particular situation, you can often attract and act in a way that will bring about the very situation you are trying to avoid. The reverse also applies in relation to inviting positive experiences into your life.

It is tempting at times to attribute cause and blame outside ourselves. However, no one else can create your experience; only you can do that. Once you understand this, you can embrace the freedom you have to choose and deliberately create the life experience you want right now. This includes deliberately creating and manifesting the experience you want with money, success, flourishing, and well-being. Do not underestimate the power of your thoughts as a powerful means of achieving the wealth you desire.

Let's look at these three vital elements in more detail.

The First Vital Element:
The Universal and Spiritual Laws

The first vital element is the Universal and Spiritual Laws that govern financial prosperity and money. These laws fall under the Universal Laws of Creation and can be used more broadly in all areas of your life. They are simple yet profound. By learning these laws, you tap into the same secrets that all masters of wealth, success, and abundance have discovered, understood, and practiced to fulfill their dreams.

Everything in our physical Universe is made of energy, and it exists in various forms. Each of us radiates our own energy. For example, when you come into contact with someone who is angry or negative, you can sense her repellent energy. The same is true of someone who is positive and happy. You are drawn to him because he has a positive and light energy.

You may have heard of the Law of Attraction: like attracts like, and your thoughts, words, and actions are mirrored back to you through your experiences (more on this law just below). Though there are other, less well-known

Universal Laws, including the Law of Least Effort, our focus in this chapter is specifically on the twelve Universal and Spiritual Laws of money and financial prosperity. So without further ado, here are the twelve Universal and Spiritual Laws of money and financial prosperity:

Law of Abundance: Abundance is your natural state. Noticing the abundance you already have in your life enables you to receive more. The opposite is also true. By only noticing what you do not have, you attract more scarcity. If you believe that you have to struggle to make money, then the way you will receive money is by struggling to generate it. Yet if you truly believe that abundance is your natural state, your experiences will naturally lead to this.

Key tip: Shift your beliefs toward abundance, and expect to experience ease and flow.

Law of Attention: Whatever you give attention to manifests, so focus on positive thoughts as often as you can. At the same time, commit to your goals and dreams, and do not overanalyze everything, because doing so can block your energy and flow. The Law of Attention concerns the focus of your thoughts, words, and actions and is closely tied to the Law of Attraction. If you give attention to worry or fear, you bring it into your experience. Therefore, watch what you focus on.

Key tip: Positive energy always has a higher and more powerful charge than negative energy, so focus on being positive as much and as often as you can.

Law of Attraction: Your experiences are affected by this law. Because what you focus your thoughts on expands, you will receive experiences that correspond with your dominant thoughts and emotions. When you think of positive things, you accelerate the process of having more positive experiences, particularly when you express gratitude for all the blessings you have already received. Once you understand this law and begin to notice what you are paying attention to, you will be able to create and shape the experiences you want in all areas of your life — including with money.

Essentially, the Law of Attraction operates on thoughts, words, emotions, and actions, which the Universe mirrors back to you through experiences. Another way to view this is that energy flows out of your body like a signal or airwave. You emit a precise signal, and only the same kind of wavelength will respond to it. The result is that you attract into your life the people and circumstances that are in alignment with what you radiate out into the world.

The Law of Attraction tends to be misunderstood as too simplistic. It is not a universal supply-and-delivery store. Rather, it is a dynamic tool to help you transform yourself to match the energy of what you want to create in your life, since like attracts like. However, the Law of Attraction cannot be used for harming others or as a remedy to magically cure a serious illness. Further, the Law of Attraction must be implemented properly. It is not enough to simply think and say what you want and then do nothing to achieve it. You must be an active participant in creating it. This means that you must be open to paying attention to the signs and opportunities that come your way, and then take the appropriate course of action.

Key tip: There is no creation without action. While having clarity is key, you must support it by taking intentional actions and being awake to the right opportunities.

Law of Clarity: When you are clear about your deepest desire and will, others respond accordingly. Whenever you are decisive and committed to a specific action, no one can stop you. One of my favorite sayings is "Never get in the way of a woman on a mission!"

On the other hand, when you lack clarity, you feel confused or frustrated, and this ties up your personal energy.

Key tip: The moment you make a clear decision that is aligned with your highest purpose, this action sends a powerful energy to the Universe, and your path lights up, allowing you to take the next step.

Law of Flow: Universal energy flows downstream, like a river. If the flow is blocked, the river overflows. This is also the case with your emotions. If you keep anger, fear, doubts, worry, and more suppressed, it is only a matter of time before your emotions overflow in negative ways. This is how your immune system can become compromised.

You will know when you are not in flow and are

heading upstream. The energy is heavy and everything feels like a burden. You are pushing to make things happen rather than enjoying the process. Your job is to make room and space for the positive flow of what you desire.

Key tip: Let go of what no longer serves you. Learn to let your emotions come to the surface and be expressed, giving them space to manifest and preventing blockages.

Law of Giving and Law of Receiving: Both these laws offer different aspects of the flow of energy. When you give what you seek, you are also keeping the flow of abundance in the Universe circulating in your life.

The beauty of giving is that it creates a vacuum and an opportunity to receive. An elegant and pure aspect of giving to others is that in truth, you are also giving to yourself. As Francis of Assisi said, "It is in giving that we receive."

Another way to take action with this law is through the spiritual practice of *tithing* — giving and donating one-tenth of the money you earn. Practicing tithing from a place of gratitude and love will result in multitudes of blessings and abundance in your life.

Key tip: While one-tenth (or 10 percent) is recommended for tithing, the exact percentage is a personal decision based on your situation. The act of giving to others does not deplete your own supply.

Law of Intention: Attaining what you desire starts with setting a clear intention. The clearer you are about your intention, the more likely it is that you will achieve what you desire. When you combine intention with taking focused action, you can manifest your desires more quickly.

One reason many of us do not realize what we want is that we are not specific enough about it. When baking a cake, you need the right ingredients and you need to follow the right steps. Otherwise, you will be making something else. It is the same thing with manifesting anything else in your life, including financial prosperity. All the right ingredients must be in place.

Once you are clear about what you want, you must take the right actions and do whatever is necessary (within reason) to achieve it.

Key tip: Once you have taken the necessary actions, surrender and release the outcome. The act of surrendering accelerates the results.

Law of Manifestation: This law is closely connected to the Law of Attraction. Manifestation is the ability to bring something into physical reality. Through the Law of Attraction, you know that what you focus on expands. As such, focusing on the positive outcomes and results that you want is vital. This includes releasing old beliefs about money that no longer serve you. The Law of Manifestation works in combination with the Law of Attraction by creating a magnet and drawing the energy of what you are focusing on to you. Therefore, it is imperative that you are crystal-clear about what you want to manifest.

Key tip: Clarity is the key to manifesting your heart's desires. The ability to manifest is a powerful skill and must only be used for the highest good.

Law of Nonattachment: Surrendering and releasing your attachment to the exact outcome you desire can be challenging. This is because, like many people, you may want to control the process. However, detaching yourself from the outcome is a critical element of manifesting your desire.

One of the ways in which we can interfere with this law is to hold on to what we already have, including our money, particularly when there is an important reason or need to spend it. Holding on to anything, in fact, blocks the free flow of energy in your life.

Mastering the Law of Nonattachment requires you to have the willingness to believe that the Universe is a place of abundance. This does not mean that you give up all your assets and everything you own. It simply means accepting that the Universe is abundant and that therefore you can create and have what you desire.

Key tip: Someone who has mastered manifestation is detached from the outcome.

Law of Prosperity: The first thought that likely comes to mind with this law is financial prosperity. While it does include money, the Law of Prosperity is much broader. Money is simply a representation or symbol of prosperity in our physical world. This law also encompasses a deep sense of abundance and well-being. This includes the be-lief that the Universe is richly abundant in all ways.

An important way to activate this law is to nurture your gifts and talents as well as to express your creativity by doing what you love through your life's work. This includes believing in and trusting yourself and your abilities. By doing so, you create a rich and fertile soil for manifesting your desires. On the other hand, a disempowered mind-set is like poor soil; it is very difficult to grow beautiful plants and vegetables in it. When you take positive actions toward nurturing the best of who you are, your prosperity will flourish.

Key tip: It does not make you more "spiritual" to keep worrying about money, because doing so blocks you from receiving your good. The most spiritual action you can take with money is to use it wisely and with love.

Law of Success: You enact this law when your personal energy resonates with the energy of your desired outcome. This law works closely with the Law of Flow; everything must be in alignment. You can be brought out of alignment when you harbor negative thoughts about yourself and your abilities. Mind-set plays an important role in achieving success (see the discussion in chapter 8). In other words, success follows when you believe in yourself.

Key tip: True success comes when you have achieved your goals through cooperation and by empowering others in the process. It can also be measured by the meaning and sense of fulfillment that your results bring you.

Law of Limitless Thinking: Positive thinking, which impacts our reality, health, and well-being, is not a new concept. Positive thoughts add to the positive energy of the entire Universe. The opposite is also true: negative thoughts add to negative energy.

A key aspect of manifesting is your willingness and ability to let go of thinking that you are missing something. Instead, take time to feel grateful for what you have already brought into your world. Most of all, joyfully embrace your ability to create, and pursue everything that you want to have and experience in your life. You can do this by being open and willing to let new and positive experiences come to you.

Key tip: Allow yourself to have more than you ever thought possible.

The Second Vital Element:
The Core Manifesting Process

The second vital element to manifesting financial prosperity and more is learning about and using the Core Manifesting Process. This process strengthens the impact of the Universal and Spiritual Laws, particularly the Law of Manifestation. You can practice this core process while starting with something small. Then as your confidence grows, you can manifest something bigger.

As you build your manifesting muscle, this process

will become easier. At some point, you will discover the best formula for you. Then you can shorten the actions within each step. However, all the steps are still needed for optimal results.

Here are the key steps:

1. **Get clear and ask.** As noted with the Law of Clarity, being clear and specific is critical because if you are not clear about what you want, you will receive modest results. You must be able to clearly answer the question, "What do I want?"

   From the point of view of the Law of Attraction, it is like ordering from the menu of the Universe. You have to ask for the exact experience you want.

   To get clear on what you want, get still, *meditate*, and listen to your inner wisdom. Then set an intention by identifying and asking for exactly what you want to bring into reality. Being intentional is powerful precisely because it requires you to be decisive. When you are decisive, the next steps become clear.

2. **Visualize receiving what you desire.** Once you have identified exactly what you want to manifest, you can begin to visualize yourself receiving what you desire in advance of having it (see the discussion on creative visualization starting on page 86).

3. **Release the outcome and have total faith.** Consistent with the Law of Nonattachment, it is essential to have a certain detachment to the outcome. Surrendering and releasing your attachments to getting the exact

outcome you desire can be challenging because most of us want to control things. But whatever is going to happen, you must truly be fine with it. Why? Because something much better that you may not even have considered could be unfolding. The Universe works in magical ways; keep in mind that you will receive what is for your *highest good* and for the highest good of others.

Once you have released the outcome, have faith that what you desire is on its way. Practicing active faith is not always easy. Practice by nurturing the feeling and acting as if you have already received what you desire, even when your experiences seem to tell you the opposite. Stand still, and keep your focus and your faith. Hold this mind-set: *ask believing, and it is already given*.

4. **Take aligned actions.** Three necessary actions are required in manifesting what you desire. The first action is to raise and *align* your personal energy with your desired outcome. This is similar to the concept of like attracts like and the Law of Attraction. One way to raise your personal energy is to enjoy the process of manifesting and to have fun. Your energy then becomes lighter. To manifest what you desire, everything must first be in alignment (see discussions in chapter 7).

The second necessary action is that you must be an active *co-creator* with Divine Source and Universal Energy to create and manifest what you desire. Since we live in a physical world, it is not enough to ask for what you want and then sit there and do nothing to create it. This is where many people get the wrong impression of the Law of Attraction. They may visualize and make a request to the Universe, but then never follow up with action. And they conclude that "it doesn't work."

The third necessary action is to *prepare* to receive what you desire and be open to taking inspired actions. For example, if you are asking for a certain amount of money, demonstrate active faith and start preparing by getting your finances in order, or open another bank account so you can create a pathway to receiving the money.

Remember: inspiration and guidance can come at any time and in many forms. If you learn best through reading a book, or writing in your journal, or being in nature, then be open to guidance from these areas.

The Third Vital Element: Key Manifesting Tools

Our focus in this section is on the four major manifesting tools that support the Core Manifesting Process — affirmations, meditation, creative visualization, and creation of your ideal scene. There are two points to keep in mind. The first is not to be fooled by the simplicity of these tools — they are powerful and transformative. Second, while the tools can be used individually, applying them in combination can help accelerate your results. You can use these tools in any area of your life, not just in creating more financial prosperity and abundance. Again, as you use these tools, you will find the best formula for you, which you can adapt to suit your style. The best part is having options.

The first major tool is the use of *affirmations*, which are positive statements and declarations that can help focus your awareness and energy to create what you want. Essentially, it is about "affirming" that what you desire is coming into reality. The quality of your words holds a tremendous power. And when repeated often enough, these words can help create your reality.

When creating your positive experiences through affirmations, here are four tips to keep in mind:

1. Create affirmations that are simple and in the present tense so you can easily repeat them. For example, *I am healthy, wealthy, and happy* or *I love my abundant life and business* or *I am now creating financial success in my business and life.*

2. Only use affirmations containing positive words that you truly believe in (even if it is a stretch and currently not your reality) so that your subconscious mind can accept them. What actually moves the needle are the energy, emotion, and intention behind the affirmation.

3. Only use affirmations that are appropriate for you and feel possible and exciting.

4. Believe that the affirmation is happening at this moment and not in the distant future, since doing so allows you to "act as if." In this way, you can experience a sense of play, lightness, and creativity, which can accelerate your results.

We will discuss the power of words and affirmations further in chapters 10 and 12.

The second major tool is *meditation*. The practice of meditation — the act of quieting the mind — has existed for thousands of years. Today meditation is used widely around the world as a form of spiritual growth, stress reduction, health and well-being management, self-improvement, and more.

When you are relaxed, sitting still, focused on your breathing, quieting your mind, and being aware in the present moment, there is a gap in time in which you are one with Divine Source and Universal Energy. It is in these moments that you can quiet the noise in your mind, receive guidance on an important next step to take, and release any resistance to manifesting your heart's desire. When you release any lingering resistance, you can more easily become aligned with your dreams. Successful creation will soon follow.

The third major tool is *creative visualization*, as taught by Shakti Gawain. Creative visualization is the technique for using your imagination to create what you desire. We all tend to imagine through pictures and images, so using your imagination is a critical manifesting tool. This is why so many people create vision boards to help them get a clear image of what they want to create.

Before we review the four steps of the creative visualization technique, I want to assure you that there's no need to worry if you cannot actually picture what you are thinking of. Everyone is different in that some people rely more on feelings and emotions or on their sense of knowing. The important thing is to harmonize the visualization with the feeling of already having what you desire. The four steps of creative visualization are:

1. **Set your goal.** Decide what you want to create and experience in any area of your life, including financial. Be clear and specific about what you desire.

2. **Create a clear idea or picture.** In as much detail as possible, imagine yourself already experiencing what you desire in the present moment.

3. **Focus on your goal often.** Focus on your mental image, and picture it clearly and as often as you can in a relaxed and light way.

4. **Give your goal positive energy.** As you focus on your goal, think of it in a positive way, see yourself achieving your goal, and use positive affirmations and statements.

The creative visualization technique is also a form of meditation in that it includes quieting your mind and focusing your thoughts in a peaceful and relaxed way.

The fourth major tool is to create your *ideal scene*, a powerful technique based on the writings and teachings of Marc Allen. It is a form of intentional dreaming and works effectively with the other three tools. Here are four steps to get you started:

1. **Imagine.** Get relaxed, close your eyes, take three deep breaths, and relax even further. Breathe in through your nose and out through your mouth.

   Imagine that five years have passed and that everything has gone very well. Ask yourself:

   What does my dream life look like?
   Where do I live?
   What am I doing? What is my life's work?
   What do I have?
   What is my financial life like?
   What are my family life and relationships like?
   How have I changed?

   Get specific, be creative, and let your imagination fly! Do not put limits on yourself and your imagination.

2. **Write it down.** Open your eyes, and write down your ideal scene. Within your ideal scene are goals. List the goals and refer to them often. This ideal scene can become your dominant vision as you see it in your mind's eye daily. You can also draw a picture or create a vision board.

3. **Develop affirmations.** Create affirmations based on the goals of your ideal scene (see tips above). As you recite your affirmations, connect emotionally with

your ideal scene as you visualize it. Generate the feeling that it is happening in the present moment.

4. **Create a plan of action.** As you integrate the ideal scene within your being, body, and subconscious, the next logical steps will appear. Then create a plan based on your intentions, and take action. Keep taking actions (big and small) toward attaining your goals and your ideal scenario.

CHAPTER SUMMARY

- Everything in the Universe is a form of energy, and all things in our physical world consist of energy, including money. All creation is a result of thought applied to the energy of action.

- The money you have and earn is a physical manifestation of what you believe you deserve.

- Your thoughts, positive or negative, create your reality — from the intangible to the tangible.

- The three vital elements related to manifesting financial prosperity and beyond include discovering the Universal and Spiritual Laws, applying the Core Manifesting Process, and using the major manifesting tools of affirmations, meditation, creative visualization, and creating the ideal scene.

- The major Universal and Spiritual Laws that can be used to manifest money, financial prosperity, and success in all areas of your life include the Law of Abundance, the Law of Attention, the

Law of Attraction, the Law of Clarity, the Law of Flow, the Law of Giving and Receiving, the Law of.Intention, the Law of Manifestation, the Law of Nonattachment, the Law of Prosperity, the Law of Success, and the Law of Limitless Thinking.

- As you build your manifesting muscle and apply the Core Manifesting Process, as well as the major tools of affirmations, meditation, creative visualization, and creating your ideal scene, take time to have fun and enjoy the art of creating. In this way you automatically raise your personal energy to one of lightness and can thus more easily attract what you desire.
- By incorporating the Universal and Spiritual Laws, you can pave the way to experiencing financial, personal, and professional success with greater joy and ease than you ever thought possible.
- In combination and as a whole, you follow the Universal and Spiritual Laws of money when you:

  - undertake your life's work while honoring and serving the higher good of yourself and others.
  - collaborate with others rather than compete with them.
  - allow every money and energy exchange to be a win-win situation for all involved.
  - spend and invest money in a way that does not harm yourself, others, or the planet.

Take Action

Bonus download at:
www.MoneyManifestationAndMiracles.com/gift

The Universal and Spiritual Laws of Money Guide Sheet

Chapter 6

TRANSFORMING YOUR RELATIONSHIP WITH MONEY

Your beliefs become your thoughts.
Your thoughts become your words.
Your words become your actions.
Your actions become your habits.
Your habits become your values.
Your values become your destiny.
— MAHATMA GANDHI

THUS FAR YOU HAVE GAINED a greater awareness of how women uniquely relate to money and why this is the best time for women to stand in their power, own their worth, and embrace the feminine connection to money. You have gained insights into your current relationship with money. You also learned about the Core Manifesting Process, the Universal and Spiritual Laws of financial prosperity, and the other major tools to bring what you desire into physical reality.

Building on the knowledge from previous chapters, you will now deepen the learning and insights with the

Eight Holistic Principles for transforming your relationship with money. In this chapter I will outline these principles, and in the next several chapters we will examine and apply them in depth.

The principles are based on the Wealth Creation System, which I developed as a way to take an integrated and holistic approach to creating meaningful wealth and prosperity in all areas of life. My eight-step system includes four essential elements. First, it enables you to embrace the belief that wealth creation is not separate from a life filled with passion, purpose, wisdom, connection to spirit, and contribution through service. Second, it is aligned with the feminine connection to money, and how we can use money to express love — taking care of ourselves and our families and sharing money to help others — to fulfill our social promise in the world.

Third, the system enables you to identify blind spots and emotional blocks that may be preventing your financial success, and equips you with the tools and strategies to address these challenges, thereby increasing your self-confidence and self-worth.

Fourth, it enables you to gain clarity on how to break free of fear and disempowering patterns regarding money so you can increase your income, impact, and success with greater ease.

Taking aligned and intentional actions is the basis for miracles. For the purposes of this book, I define miracles as "the alignment of your highest self with your highest purpose, combined with the implementation of

Universal Laws and inspired actions to create extraordinary results."

The operative word in this definition is *action*; you don't want to let opportunities pass you by. By consciously taking action to transform your relationship with money, you can experience:

- a healthier and more enjoyable way to create and relate to money so you can finally have emotional peace with money.
- an ability to accelerate your personal and spiritual growth so you can help many more people through your life's work.
- a better way to pursue personal fulfillment by doing what you love and by leveraging money and wealth to make a meaningful social impact on the world.
- a life of *true wealth* and prosperity so that you can enjoy an abundant lifestyle, one with greater flow and ease.

If you are wondering what *true wealth* and prosperity can look like in your own life, here are six aspects of true wealth and prosperity that you can adopt (or feel free to create your own criteria):

1. A richness of love and joy in your relationship with yourself and the Divine Source, or however you choose to identify God
2. Vitality in your physical health and overall well-being (body, mind, and soul)

3. Passion for doing what you love so that it feels like play
4. Satisfying, nurturing, honest, and authentic relationships
5. Generating income that supports your highest purpose and spiritual path
6. Having the money to lead a life of quality and meaning

The six aspects of *true wealth* and prosperity are also incorporated in the Transforming Your Relationship with Money diagram below.

It Begins with You

Starting with the interior circle of the diagram, the most central element to the whole success equation of your work and life is you. Simply put, you are the source of all your wealth, happiness, and abundance. Your capacity to manifest your vision, dreams, and goals into reality all begins with you. After all, you are the CEO and leader of your life.

The first circle also takes into consideration that you bring a broad range of experiences to your interaction with money. These encounters have influenced and shaped how you think and feel about money. Your family imprinting as well as cultural and social conditioning regarding money is all part of what makes you who you are today and what influences your relationship to money.

Your Successful Relationship with Money

The second circle of the diagram is devoted to creating your successful relationship with money.

Now is the time to shift your precious energy away from what is keeping you stuck and instead use this energy toward transforming yourself. The key method to transforming yourself is through awareness, clarity, and an understanding of your relationship with money, since these things are the gateway to a future of more financial prosperity, freedom, and fulfillment.

The Eight Holistic Principles

The third circle focuses on each of the Eight Holistic Principles. The principles are the foundation for developing an empowered and optimal relationship with money. Each of the principles builds on the others, and when combined, can be applied effectively to generating financial prosperity and enduring wealth.

Clarity

The principle of clarity is the starting point of your inner journey, enabling you to create a new and more empowered relationship with money. It will also increase your ability to manifest wealth and abundance in your life's work. The focus of this step is to create clarity through self-knowledge and awareness and to help you with:

- gaining an understanding of who you are (self-knowledge).
- discerning your core personal values as they relate to your life and work.
- honoring your value and self-worth in relation to your talents and gifts and the compensation you receive for your work.
- having a realistic and optimistic view of yourself and your true potential.
- clearly identifying and visualizing what you want to manifest and experience in your life.
- having trust and faith in yourself and your abilities.

- understanding how money plays out (positively or negatively) in your work, finances, relationships, and so on.
- identifying and setting meaningful money goals (i.e., being clear about what you want).

Mind-Set and Beliefs

Everything starts with mind-set. Your mind-set influences your beliefs and actions. Other words used to describe mind-set include *beliefs*, *thoughts*, *viewpoint*, *paradigm*, *mentality*, and *attitudes*. The focus of this principle is on shifting limiting beliefs and assumptions regarding money to ones that are more positive, thereby enabling you to create a more harmonious relationship with money. Often the reason you are not able to create this harmonious relationship is that you have a mental block that keeps you from taking action.

Emotions

Money conjures up many emotions for people. Each of us has our own emotional triggers. The focus of this principle is on releasing your emotional blocks to wealth. This includes facing common emotions — fears, doubts, shame, guilt, and anger regarding money — and not backing away from these intense feelings or avoiding them. The key to transformational change is to get to the root cause of the emotions. It then becomes easier to pursue the right course of action so you can move forward more intentionally. Once you address limiting beliefs and emotional blocks to wealth, you will become unstoppable in achieving personal and professional fulfillment, financial freedom, and the success you desire.

Self-Expression

Often we do not realize how powerful we really are in what we say and how we talk about money. How you express yourself can ultimately create your experiences and reality, both positive and negative.

Therefore, the focus of this principle is to help you express yourself and communicate about money in a more positive and optimistic way. This will, in turn, affect the quality of your conversations with your colleagues, clients, customers, bank, life partner, family, friends, and more.

Purpose and Impact

This principle is based on creating complete alignment between who you are and your purpose and passion. It is also based on the alignment between your actions and the impact you want to make with your greater "why" regarding money. For many women, the answer to the question of "why," as it pertains to wealth, often does not come easily. The main reason for this, as we have seen, is that for women money is not as straightforward as it is for men. It is more ambiguously connected to emotions, relationships, and meaning.

The good news is that because of this reality, you will be more able to generate income once you connect your greater "why" and purpose with money. Knowing your deeper purpose can function as an anchor and deepen your connection with money, since it will act as the motivator behind why you are doing what you are doing. Having this anchor will be especially valuable when you are experiencing moments of doubt, fear, and frustration, all common emotions on the road to success.

Actions

The principle of action focuses on empowering your behavior and habits regarding money, which includes integrity, self-responsibility, and accountability.

This principle helps you align your habits and actions regarding money to ones that are more productive and healthier. When you are in alignment, you will be able to end self-sabotaging actions in relation to money that cause you to give away your power and decrease your self-confidence.

Environment

The principle of environment focuses on surrounding yourself with people who will support you in creating a harmonious and abundant relationship with money so that you can experience the financial freedom, fulfillment, and success you desire. This principle also focuses on putting yourself in an optimal setting for wealth and success.

Focus

The principle of focus concentrates on two key areas. The first is to pay attention to your money and financial activities. The second is to concentrate on taking steps to achieve your desired monetary goals by eliminating unnecessary distractions from your mind-set, your interactions with others, and your environment. Essentially it is about making your goals your top priority. It is also about taking intentional and consistent actions to achieve these goals.

Now that we are equipped with the background, in the rest of the chapters we will take an in-depth look at these Eight Holistic Principles.

CHAPTER SUMMARY

- The Eight Holistic Principles for Transforming Your Relationship with Money are based on the Wealth Creation System. The system takes an integrated and holistic approach to creating wealth, prosperity, and abundance in all areas of your life.
- The holistic approach enables you to transform your relationship with money and enhances your sense of abundance, self-confidence, and self-worth. The Wealth Creation System is designed to help you identify blind spots and emotional blocks that may be holding you back from financial success. The system also equips you with the strategies and tools to address these blocks, which will increase your self-confidence and self-worth.

- Taking action to heal and address disempowering patterns with money can help you to dramatically increase your income, impact, and success. It can also help you experience an abundant life of financial prosperity, freedom, fulfillment, and contribution.

- The Eight Holistic Principles diagram incorporates the understanding that wealth creation is not separate from a life filled with passion, purpose, wisdom, connection to spirit, and making a contribution through service.

- You are the single most important element to the success equation of your life because you are the source of all your wealth, happiness, and abundance.

- Your capacity to manifest your vision, dreams, and goals begins with you.

Take Action

Bonus download at:
www.MoneyManifestationAndMiracles.com/quiz

The Wealth Creation Assessment: pinpoint blind spots and identify solutions for more financial prosperity.

Part 3

A HOLISTIC
APPROACH

Chapter 7

Holistic Principle 1

CLARITY LEADS TO ALIGNMENT

Knowing yourself is the beginning of all wisdom.
— ARISTOTLE

YOU ARE THE CEO AND THE LEADER of your life and your life's work. Yet maybe you are not quite feeling like the hero of your life story, and that's all right. You are not alone. The beautiful reality is that you have chosen to accelerate your personal and spiritual journey by empowering your relationship with money. I believe that the path leads first to gaining an inner understanding of yourself. I also believe that the keys to abundance are already within you. In fact, the keys to prosperity have always been within you because abundance is your natural state.

The focus of this chapter is on the holistic principle of clarity and on helping you get into alignment with the best of who you are by tapping into your values and your strengths. This alignment further enables you to more fully honor your self-worth. We are also building on our discussion regarding the Law of Clarity in chapter 5, and specifically the benefits of being crystal-clear about your deepest desire as an important strategy for manifesting that desire.

Once you have tapped into your values and strengths, the next step is to align them with the meaning of money and to set meaningful monetary goals.

Aligning with Your True Desires

I cannot overstate the importance of being in alignment with who you are and everything you do. When you are in alignment, everything flows; life feels easy; and opportunities, including people, money, and resources, will show up on your doorstep to help you achieve your goals. When you are in alignment, you are also at your best and most joyful. When you are in a state of joy, your personal energy is stronger, enabling you to more quickly manifest what you desire. This includes manifesting financial prosperity and abundance in all its forms.

Likewise, it is harder to achieve what you desire when you are out of alignment, when things just do not seem to go your way, with many blocks and obstacles to overcome. We have all experienced this at some point. Earlier on, I noted that I have found the main reasons that women are not doing as well as they could be. Some factors that hold women back from greater success relate to a disconnection between:

- what they have accomplished and their level of self-confidence
- what they really want and what they settle for
- valuing what they do and valuing their self-worth
- the determination they show on the outside and the fear and doubt they have about themselves on the inside

The disconnection stems from being out of alignment with themselves and their truth. This is why self-knowledge is so vital; it provides you with awareness and clarity. And having clarity crystallizes what actions you need to take to get aligned with what you desire. The reverse is also true. When you get into alignment, you gain greater clarity. Either way, it's all good.

So what are the blocks to gaining self-knowledge? There are three main ones:

Self-Knowledge Block 1. Being unaware of your personal values: You may not have revisited your values in a while, or maybe you've never taken the opportunity to discover them in the first place. Many goal-oriented women often do not have the time to stop and "smell the roses." You may always be on the go, without ever stopping to think about the following: what truly fulfills you, what brings you the greatest meaning and joy, what you most cherish, and what you would take a stand on.

Self-Knowledge Block 2. Not fully embracing your natural strengths: First of all, do you know what your natural strengths even are? If you do not, a simple exercise in this chapter on the three steps to embrace your natural strengths can help you get started. Your natural strengths come very easily to you — just like breathing. You may even take your strengths for granted. This is a common habit because we have been taught from an early age to work on our weaknesses rather than nurturing our strengths. However, when we take the time to nurture our strengths, we accelerate our growth and success.

Self-Knowledge Block 3. Being unclear about your life's purpose and how to express it in your work and personal life: Your life's purpose, or your calling, is unique to you. When you are unclear about your purpose, it contributes to being out of alignment with your full potential. However, when you are connected to your purpose, it can bring you a sense of deep fulfillment and direction in your life. (See the discussion in chapter 11, where we will dive even deeper into aligning your purpose with the impact you want to make on the world.)

There is a reason you chose to read this book, and now is the perfect time to revisit these blockages and release them. Seeking advice from your trusted friends is a natural thing to do when you feel like you are straying from your path. However, your friends may not be sure themselves as to how to reconnect you with your values or help you discover, or rediscover, your life's purpose. They themselves may not be aware of their own life's purpose or sure how to find it. Other reasons your friends might not be the best people to advise you could be that they are simply too busy leading their own hectic lives or that they are not on the same path as you. As such, it is often beneficial to obtain the support of a professional coach or mentor who has the training and insight to know what questions to ask you, and who will possess the tools to help you express your purpose with grace and ease.

Shine Your Light

I find it truly inspiring when women are empowered and wholeheartedly own their brilliance and strengths, with no apologies. When you are truly empowered, you can achieve so much and make such a meaningful difference, in your unique way. This is because you are in alignment with all that you are and all that you do in the world.

It is time to embrace your special strengths and personal values. Some people refer to them as your "God-given talents." We all possess strengths and nonstrengths (what many refer to as "weaknesses"). I am a supporter of the concept of flourishing — focusing your energy on nurturing and celebrating your strengths rather than trying to "fix" your flaws. The results are so much more rewarding, the biggest one being what positive psychology pioneer Dr. Martin Seligman calls "authentic happiness."

Here is a simple exercise on the three steps to embrace your natural strengths:

Exercise: Embracing Your Natural Strengths

Step 1. Using your journal, think about a specific moment when you felt deeply engaged or fulfilled. What was going on? What made this moment special? (Remember to be specific in your response by using examples.)

Step 2. What strengths were you accessing in yourself at that time?

Step 3. Highlight and list the key strengths that resonate for you.

In reflecting on your responses, answer these questions:

- What came up for you?
- Are you surprised? If so, why?
- What specific actions will you take to incorporate your strengths more often in your work and in other areas of life?

Uncovering Your Value System

Let us now focus on uncovering your personal values. Your values are what make you tick. They reflect the core of who you are in your life right now. Remember, your values do not reflect who you want to be or who you think you must be. They are authentic to you, and as such, there is no need to change them. Your values affect all areas of your life. It is not necessary to differentiate between your work and the rest of your life, since it all matters. Your values serve as a compass to guide you to get into alignment with your decisions and actions in all areas, including money.

A key way to know whether you are in alignment is by conducting a small test. When making a decision, check in with how you are feeling. Usually if the decision is not in alignment with your values, your intuition will kick in, and it will just not feel right. However, when you choose to ignore these signs — which we have all done at some point — you will likely encounter some type of drama and struggle in your experiences.

Here is a strategy to help you identify and clarify your values. Using your journal, begin by identifying a specific moment in your life when you felt most fulfilled and joyful. It can be the same example used in the previous exercise, or you can choose a new one. Be sure to choose a specific moment when you were at your best and in complete alignment. Using this specific example, answer the following questions:

- What values were you honoring in this moment?
- What makes these values so important to you?
- How do you feel when you are honoring these values?
- *How* and *where* do these values show up in your work and life right now?

In all likelihood you came up with more than ten values that are of importance. You can identify as many values as you would like. In reviewing them, choose your top five. These top five values are the most important ones for you to nurture, incorporate, and express in your life's work.

Honor Your Self-Worth

For women, the topic of self-worth cuts to the core of what we truly believe we can do. It also cuts to the core of your attitude toward yourself and your level of self-respect. These all impact your self-confidence and self-esteem. The topic of self-worth also gets to the essence of what triggers your emotions when it comes to money (we'll discuss this in more detail in chapter 9). Each of the principles and exercises in this book has been building on the others to help you gain greater self-confidence, empower your relationship with money, and increase your self-appreciation. As a whole, the holistic principles that we will be discussing over the next chapters will support you in embracing your self-worth. For now, when it comes to self-worth and prosperity, here are four keys to keep in mind:

Prosperity Key 1. Your self-worth must rise with your net worth.

Prosperity Key 2. You must believe that you can be financially prosperous and wealthy.

Prosperity Key 3. You must believe that you can ask for

more in your life, and be unafraid to back this belief up with actions.

Prosperity Key 4. You must be ready to take advantage of the opportunities you encounter.

Incorporating these keys to prosperity is a vital part of the work I do with my clients, since I have found that many women entrepreneurs have difficulty charging and getting paid for the value of their important work. I have also found that many women have difficulty asking for a raise or negotiating their salaries. As a result, they are disappointed with what they earn. This, in turn, affects their confidence and self-esteem. This dynamic often leads to a cycle of self-blame and disharmony, which needless to say, does not promote success.

I have also found that some women feel they have to reduce their fees to get more clients, or simply not ever raise their fees. In effect, they are cutting off the flow of money to themselves, creating resentment and frustration. Later in the book we will discuss further what factors lead women to engage in self-sabotaging actions and ways to address them. Overcoming these disempowering patterns of behavior is essential to helping you feel more empowered with money.

Here are seven truths that can help you shift your mind-set about your self-worth so that you can increase your net worth in your business, career, and life:

Self-Worth Truth 1. When you undervalue yourself and what you do, others will also undervalue you.

Self-Worth Truth 2. When you value your services and expertise, others will value them too.

Self-Worth Truth 3. When you value your services and expertise, you feel more comfortable charging what you are worth and receiving suitable compensation for your expertise.

Self-Worth Truth 4. If you are a business owner, it is vital to love what you do and to love your clients or customers. Just do not confuse this with providing discounts or free services or products on an ongoing basis.

Self-Worth Truth 5. In order to be at your best, you have to maintain your energy and motivation at a high level. As such, it is best to work with clients, customers, and companies who are the right fit. You do not have to feel obligated to work with everyone.

Self-Worth Truth 6. Honoring your self-worth includes valuing your time, boundaries, talents, and expertise.

Self-Worth Truth 7. Focus your expertise on a specific niche area and become an expert in that field or topic. When you are an expert, you are able to charge more.

A Bonus Tip

A key way to honor your worth is to offer your services only to those who will value them, since they are more likely to benefit; to use your efforts for their highest good;

and to help others. In this way you contribute to a positive ripple effect.

HILLARY'S STORY

Hillary is a career and talent coach who loves helping her clients land the vocation of their dreams. She works with both women and men but has found that she has coached more women about negotiating their salary or raise.

She wanted to work with me because she felt like she was a fraud. When we peeled back the layers, Hillary admitted that while she felt great about helping her clients feel more confident and empowered with doing what they love and making great money, she was not practicing what she was preaching.

Hillary was not honoring herself and her self-worth. Deep within, she was experiencing an inner conflict about valuing her time, expertise, and boundaries. She cared so much for her clients that she would go over time in her sessions and often provide discounts when they requested them, thinking this was the best way to stay competitive in her market.

She was also attracting more clients who were high-maintenance and who made unnecessary demands. They referred their colleagues to her because she was a great coach who charged bargain prices. Hillary began to feel resentful toward some clients, and she also blamed herself, which is not what she wanted to create in her business. It was time to make a change.

Through our work, she reconnected with her personal values and strengths and began to own her self-worth. She realized the great value of her work of guiding people to change the course of their careers. For many this was priceless. She finally realized that she needed to focus on the amazing value she provided and let her pricing reflect this rather than focusing on providing bargain prices.

Hillary became very clear on the value she provides, revised her pricing and packaging structure, and tightened her boundaries. As a result, she no longer goes overtime or provides reduced rates, and she says no when people ask for discounts, works with action-oriented and motivated clients, and focuses on providing the best value to her clients. She is happy and thriving in her business.

Name and Claim Your Money Goal

Setting meaningful goals is critical in helping you move toward your money and income goal(s). The central question to ask when setting a money goal is: "How much do I really want to make?" Using your journal, write your money goal for the year and fill in the blank. Your money goal can relate to the income you want to earn.

My big money goal for this year is _____.

How do you feel about the amount you just wrote down? Are you excited? Does it feel doable? Keep in mind that you are not alone. Setting a big money goal can cause many women to reduce the amount of the goal for fear of not being able to achieve it. Conversely, others may set a goal that is too high or ambitious.

Try to arrive at a middle ground when choosing a money goal for yourself. Remember, it has to feel possible and also be a reasonable stretch. Also keep in mind that your money goal is related to your mind-set. Always let your prosperity reflect the good you contribute to the world. As I've said before, it is not more spiritual or nobler to be poor, for money is often required to accomplish your life's work. Just imagine what you can accomplish!

ERIN'S STORY

Erin is the founder of a live-event company. Her clients include small business owners, experts, and authors. She also provides services to her favorite charities and fundraisers. It is a competitive and creative industry in which she feels at home.

The good news is that Erin loves her business and really enjoys her work. She has a great reputation and made over six figures in the past two years. The not-so-good news is that Erin finds it challenging to identify her next big money goal because she thinks, "Why change a good thing? Being in the six-figure zone is great." Yet, she also wants to grow her business even more. So Erin felt both scared to stretch her comfort zone and excited to step up her game and try to expand her horizons.

When we began working together, Erin had a hard time answering this simple question: "How much do you really want to make?" She took a long time to answer, as if she were afraid to say the wrong thing.

The best way to start is to bite the bullet and just get started. And that's what we did. Erin's dream money goal is to make $550,000 in the next year. This represents almost three times her current income. We then made an assessment of how realistic this was in her business. Although ambitious, half a million dollars is certainly possible to achieve; however, Erin would have to adjust her business model and hire more team members, which she was not ready to do. So while this number definitely stretched her comfort zone, it wasn't feasible for her at this stage of her growth.

Taking all things into account, Erin arrived at her true income goal for the year: $300,000. It both represented a stretch for her and helped Erin get excited about the possibilities of serving more people, without feeling overwhelmed or anxious by stretching herself too thin. We then worked on adjusting Erin's revenue streams, services, packages, pricing, and rollout plan to keep her on track for achieving her big money goal. Erin also committed to using the Core Manifesting Process and creative visualization.

Now that you have identified and claimed your big money goal, it is time to nurture this important intention. This is where the manifesting tools discussed in chapter 5 will be especially valuable. This includes using affirmations, meditating, creative visualization, and creating your ideal scene with money. As you take combined actions on a consistent basis, manifesting your goal into physical reality will follow.

It's Safe to Trust Yourself

Even when you are receptive to change, it is still normal to feel some fear of the unknown. It is common for feelings of self-doubt and fear to surface when you begin to stretch beyond your comfort zone and make meaningful changes in your life, particularly when it comes to money. Everyone can relate to this. The biggest obstacle you will experience comes from within you. It comes in the form of a persistent, negative inner voice that is critical and judgmental, often sending messages such as "I'm not good enough" or "I will be humiliated if I fail." While we all have some form of Inner Critic, we need to remember that we also have the ability to develop our inner resources and inner strength, which are more powerful than any fear.

A helpful way to tame your anxieties and doubts is to adopt more positive habits that are consistent with the best of who you are. One way to adopt more positive habits is by developing trust in yourself. Doing so will help you overcome your Inner Critic. Self-trust comes from having an optimistic and realistic belief in your true potential. When you have a high level of trust and faith in yourself and your abilities, you will feel more resourceful. You will be more willing to take on challenges and risks in order to realize your dreams, despite having fears. Another important way of supporting and believing in yourself is to ask for help when you need it. This is not easy for many women because we are natural multitaskers. But just because we can do a million things at once doesn't mean that we have to! To get more support, it can be especially important to seek the help of a professional as well as to be part of an optimal environment where others are also thriving (see the discussion about healthy community in chapter 13).

My clients frequently ask me how to tame their Inner Critic. These are my recommendations:

1. Accept your Inner Critic because some form of it will always be with you.

2. Befriend your Inner Critic by using humor to diffuse its importance. This will allow you to shift your energy into finding positive — and even fun — ways to manage your Inner Critic effectively. I created an exercise called Six Steps to Befriending Your Inner Critic for Good!, which you can download at the end of this chapter.

Above all, remember that you are in charge of your destiny. Whatever your past or current challenges with money are, they do not define who you are or dictate your future.

CHAPTER SUMMARY

- Before you start down the path to mastering money, you must first cultivate an understanding of yourself.
- One of the objectives of this book is to reconnect you with who you really are, and have always been — a creative, resourceful, and powerful individual. This is your natural state, free from any attachment to self-doubts and self-imposed limitations.
- The keys to prosperity, wealth, and abundance are already within you.
- Embracing your strengths and personal values will bring you into alignment with the best of who you are and everything that you do. When you are in alignment, everything flows and feels easy. When you are at your joyful best, opportunities, resources, and people show up to help you achieve your goals.
- We all possess strengths and nonstrengths. Focus your energy on nurturing, developing, and celebrating your strengths rather than trying to "fix" your nonstrengths. The results are much more rewarding.
- In order for you to become prosperous, your self-worth must rise with your net worth. You must

also believe that you can be wealthy, that you deserve to be prosperous, and that you can ask for more in your life. Don't be afraid to back up these beliefs with action.

- When setting your money goal, choose an amount that feels possible for you and also represents a reasonable and exciting stretch. Remember to let your prosperity reflect the good you contribute to the world.

- Once you claim your big money goal, it is vital to nurture it through various manifesting tools, including affirmations, meditation, creative visualization, and creating your ideal scene.

- It is common to experience self-doubt and fears when stretching beyond your comfort zone. The biggest obstacle in moving forward comes from within us, in the form of our Inner Critic. Understand that you can leverage your strengths and inner resources, which are more powerful than any fear.

Take Action

Bonus download at:

www.MoneyManifestationAndMiracles.com/gift

Six Steps to Befriending Your Inner Critic for Good!

Chapter 8

Holistic Principle 2

YOUR MIND-SET
MATTERS MOST

*Within you right now is the power to do things
you never dreamed possible. This power becomes available
to you just as soon as you can change your beliefs.*
— MAXWELL MALTZ

IN THIS CHAPTER our focus is on the holistic principle of belief and mind-set. Your mind-set shapes all your experiences. Whether your state of mind is fixed or open to change determines what you will experience in the world. Your mind is constantly monitoring and interpreting every moment of your experience. This is the case for all of us. We look for clues in our external world to validate our existing assumptions and belief systems. This applies to every area of our lives, including money.

The topic of mind-set is vast and must not be underestimated. It is widely discussed and taught by various professionals in the field of personal development and human potential as a way to help people shift their beliefs, energy, and actions to create a new reality. In fact, influential books on mind-set, motivation, and personal development, such as *Think and Grow Rich* by Napoleon Hill, *The Science of Getting Rich* by Wallace D. Wattles, and Ernest Holmes's *The Science of Mind*, which were written more than half a century ago, are widely used as important resources and inspiration.

In my work with clients, I focus on helping them to harmonize and align their mind-sets with the best version of who they are and with their intentions and actions. Put simply, the quality of your mind-set — your thoughts, beliefs, viewpoint, and attitude toward money — is critical to your success in achieving the financial prosperity you desire.

Mind-Set Is the Prelude to Action

Your mind-set is the driving force behind your decisions, and the prelude to your actions. The following quote from Henry Ford, founder of Ford Motor Company, captures the significance of mind-set: "Whether you think you can or whether you think you can't, you're right."

As you will note from the Mind-Set Flow diagram

below, your mind-set influences your beliefs, impacts your emotions, and affects your decisions and actions.

Mind-Set Flow

Mind-Set ➡ Influences Beliefs ➡ Impacts Emotions ➡ Affects Decisions and Actions

The Mind-Set Flow diagram also works in the reverse order. For example, your decisions and actions impact your emotions, influence your beliefs, and affect your mind-set.

Let us now take a closer look at the topic of mind-set in relation to money. You have likely heard the term *wealth consciousness* in reference to money. Wealth consciousness encompasses much more than just generating money. Wealth consciousness also includes viewing life with ease and not as a struggle, understanding that being grateful opens up more opportunities to be grateful for, and recognizing deep within that everything you need is available. These qualities are the opposite of poverty consciousness, which is rooted in the mind-set of scarcity and lack.

Taking the Mind-Set Flow diagram a step further in relation to money, the Money Mind-Set Cycle below illustrates how your mind-set, emotions, beliefs, decisions, and actions are part of an overall cycle in which you can either experience success or struggle with money. This cycle can perpetuate the same experiences and money drama over and over until you decide to change it.

Money Mind-Set Cycle

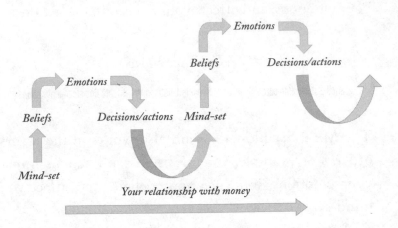

Your relationship with money

To be fair, no one is immune from having disempowering and limiting thoughts and beliefs, even if their nature is normally positive and optimistic. What matters most is what you do when you experience the thoughts and beliefs that hold you back. Ultimately, there is no one definition of a money mind-set. It is really about what you believe about yourself and what you think is possible in terms of money and wealth.

Your Money Beliefs Are Running Your Income

As we have seen, both women and men harbor many beliefs about money that originate from childhood, social conditioning, and life experiences. More often than not these beliefs come from a place of lack rather than abundance.

One common belief is: "Money is the root of all evil."

However, this is a reinterpretation of the original phrase from the Bible, which is: "The love of money is the root of all evil." People who believe that money itself is evil usually want to distance themselves from money. As a result, they have an internal resistance to earning it, saving it, managing it, or handling it.

Another common belief is that money is scary. Having money, investments, and assets can be frightening and threatening for some people. These fears likely stem from past experiences of feeling uneasy about being perceived as wealthy, of having family and friends asking for loans, or feeling victimized regarding money. They likely want to stay under the radar, and perhaps be underearners, finding this easier than being vulnerable to being envied for their wealth or to being defrauded.

For women, I have found four key money beliefs that can hold them back from moving to the next level in their professional growth. The first common belief is: "It's not about the money. I just want to help lots of people." There is an underlying belief that making more money is selfish, greedy, and/or not spiritual. Often the result is that these individuals are underearning and overgiving in their work, leading to burnout and resentment. If this is the case for you, please understand that generating more money through your life's work enables you to reach more people. It is a synergistic flow. Money provides you with more choices to fuel the mission you are passionate about creating; to enjoy a better quality of life for yourself and your family; and to fund your social promise by, for example, contributing to a favorite cause.

The second commonly held belief that can hold women back is: "I have to have everything in place before I can take the next big step." This concept is closely tied to being a perfectionist and becoming distracted with what others are doing. This can lead to thinking that more training is required or that you need to obtain more credentials before fully stepping up in your work, promoting yourself, being more visible, and becoming a leader.

The third common belief is: "I can't make more than I did in my previous position." This is particularly the case with businesswomen who have had a high level of success in their past jobs. There is an underlying assumption that they may not be able to repeat their previous standard of achievement. The internal dialogue includes questions such as "What if I fail?" and "What will people think of me?" In some cases, these women have created a ceiling for themselves, thinking they can never break it. In truth, as a businesswoman, you have an opportunity to make more money than ever before. This can happen when you give yourself permission to make more, and when you are willing to break free of your limiting, self-sabotaging beliefs.

The fourth common belief is: "My clients won't pay that much" or "I can't ask for a raise in my job." If this rings true for you, this may stem from some form of undervaluing yourself, your skills, and the value and benefits you provide, which can prevent you from charging and getting paid what you are worth. This can be an unproductive cycle that can impact your self-confidence. The reality is that it is not our place to make decisions for someone else. When you are aligned and empowered with who you are and the value you provide, your ideal clients or customers will be those who also value the investment they are making in themselves by working with you. This also extends to feeling confident about requesting a raise in your job because doing so expresses the value and contribution you provide to the organization.

MIRANDA'S STORY

Miranda is a small-business e-commerce start-up coach for women. She has a background in product design and marketing. Miranda enjoys her business and loves working with creative and innovative clients.

She sought me out because she wanted to take her business to the next income bracket and was not sure how to make it happen. In exploring different target markets, Miranda was not interested in considering the market of serving "mompreneurs"— women who juggle being both mothers and entrepreneurs. She thought that they would not have time to devote to their business and that they may not be able to pay her fees.

During our work together, Miranda was able to challenge her assumptions and her resistance. It turns out that when she was younger, her mother started her own bakery business but was unable to make it work while also balancing care of three young kids. She also had a lack of funds. This experience had stayed with Miranda.

As Miranda began to shift her mind-set, she realized that the mompreneur industry is both huge and profitable. She also realized that the e-commerce business model is an excellent fit with mompreneurs because it allows them greater flexibility in their lives. In general, as well, these women love to share and to create innovative ways to help other mothers and their children thrive.

Miranda successfully expanded her target audience, reach, and business to include mompreneurs. She is thrilled with the results and loves helping these women turn their creativity into innovative solutions for other parents and families.

In nurturing a positive mind-set, you will need to be in an environment with like-minded people who are successful and wealthy, because this will help motivate you. They can serve as role models, demonstrating that you too can have success. The key element is for you to fully show up and play a much bigger game in your business or career. The best way to accomplish this is by shifting your money mind-set to one that is more empowering.

Reset Your Money Beliefs

The good news is that you can shift your mind-set much more easily than you may think. This is especially the case when you are open and willing to learn and grow from every experience (both good and bad), as well as when you have the desire to improve (you can also download the Money Beliefs Breakthrough exercise at the end of the chapter). One step toward making this shift is to simply recognize that you have the ability and the power to choose at any moment. And in order to create a more empowered reality, you must first make the shift from within.

Your beliefs are assumptions you have made about your reality. And naturally, we look for evidence to support our beliefs. For example, if you believe that the world is abundant, you will look for evidence that this is so and act in a way that aligns with this assumption. Not surprisingly, more often than not, your experiences will match your point of view.

From the perspective of manifesting, if you believe that you will make money only for working very hard, then this will be the case for you. Perhaps you fear that having a larger sum of money will be a burden for you, causing too much responsibility. Whatever the case, if you want to change your experiences, you must change your beliefs. As you begin this process, ask yourself: "What do I have to believe to create the situation or experience that I desire?"

Keep in mind that whatever you focus on expands. Therefore, you will receive even more thoughts of the same type, be they positive or negative. Once again, the choice is yours. Abundance is your natural state, so when you hold on to negative thoughts and energy, you are expending more energy to resist the flow of abundance that is already present and occurs naturally in your life. Using your journal, answer the following questions and imagine unleashing the power of positive thinking in terms of money, specifically your money:

• What possibilities open up for you?
• What do you now choose to believe about money?
• What beliefs are you willing to change?
• What actions are you willing to take?

Letting Go of Resistance

As you begin the process of shifting those beliefs and assumptions about money that no longer serve you, let go of any residual resistance you may have toward making more money.

Among my clients I have observed a common lingering resistance to letting go of being a victim of fate or circumstance. Though these women may not consciously think of themselves as victims, their unconscious beliefs have led them to create situations in their work and life that embody this identity.

FIONA'S STORY

Fiona is a brilliant engineer and systems-project-management consultant.

She wanted to get to the root of why she was stuck at her income ceiling and unable to get to the next level. She was talented and well respected in her field as an expert. Her predicament puzzled her.

In our work together, Fiona shared that she was recovering from breast cancer, was feeling really down, and could not seem to secure any new contracts. She had invested a lot of money in training and certifications, but nothing seemed to work. She was angry with herself and with others for the position she found herself in.

Fiona was finding ways to distract herself from fully showing up in her work. Her breakthrough came when I asked her to let go of her victim identity. It was time to let go of it for good, so she could let success and abundance flow in.

She appeared shocked at first. There was a long silence, then tears. And then a breakthrough. Fiona's body language changed dramatically, and her posture and demeanor shifted from one of defeat and frustration to one of clarity and insight. She finally got it!

Fiona had been carrying her family's victim identity — especially from the women in her family. She brought into reality the very fear she voiced to relatives and friends over the years. Her deepest fear was having the same illness that her grandmother, her mother, and two of her five aunts had developed. They all developed breast cancer. Since being diagnosed, Fiona identified with being a victim of her circumstance, which leaked into all areas of her life. The profound realization for Fiona is that unlike her grandmother, mother, and aunts, she survived. The victim identity was no longer serving her.

Through our work, Fiona was finally able to break free of her resistance and disempowering beliefs in order to heal the past and successfully release the victim identity for good. Within one week after our session, Fiona secured a sizable contract. She continues to thrive.

CHAPTER SUMMARY

- Mind-set plays a vital role in our experiences, since it influences our beliefs, impacts our emotions, and affects our decisions and actions. Mind-set is the prelude to and starting point for all actions.

- The mind-set that brought you to this point is not the same mind-set you will need in advancing to your desired next level. A new set of beliefs, thoughts, habits, and actions is required to move you forward.

- Everything that exists in your life right now is what you believe you deserve. In other words, to know what you believe, look at what you have.

- You can increase your financial prosperity and wealth by shifting the way you think about money.

- In order to live a wealthy life on the outside, you must start on the inside — specifically with your mind-set, thoughts, and beliefs. To change your reality, you must first change your thoughts.

- Ultimately, mind-set is really about what you believe is possible for you.

- Remember, mind-set can be shifted more easily than you may think. An initial step toward change is to recognize that you have the ability and power to choose at any given moment.
- Believing that you can be wealthy and abundant is vital. Often all that stands between you and the money you desire is a lack of conviction. Start believing that you can achieve it, because you can.
- It is essential to cultivate wealth consciousness — a belief that involves viewing life with ease and not as a struggle, being grateful and open to an abundance of opportunities, and knowing that there is an unlimited supply of prosperity to support all your financial and spiritual needs. This process includes expanding your wealth consciousness by accepting that the world is abundant.
- What begins to show up in your experiences and reality matches your mind-set and belief. Therefore, it is critical to cultivate wealth consciousness.

Take Action

Bonus download at:
www.MoneyManifestationAndMiracles.com/gift
Money Beliefs Breakthrough Exercise

Chapter 9

Holistic Principle 3

HEAL YOUR EMOTIONS ABOUT MONEY

If you get the inside right, the outside will fall into place.
— ECKHART TOLLE

THE TOPIC OF MONEY is passionately charged, and each of us has our own emotional triggers when it comes to money. I am sure you have heard stories of or even personally experienced situations in which families, marriages, partnerships, and friendships have thrived or crumbled because of an issue concerning money.

This chapter focuses on the holistic principle of emotion and helping you to release emotional blocks to accumulating the wealth you deserve. In order to do so, as you've seen, you must first identify your disempowering feelings regarding money. You then have a beautiful opportunity to face any self-limiting feelings and emotions regarding money and not back away from them. The key is to get to the root cause of your self-sabotaging attitudes and then take the right efforts to address them so you can move forward with greater joy and ease.

There is power to your feelings, which are closely tied to your beliefs. The emotions you have regarding financial prosperity and wealth come from your beliefs about money. For example, if you really do not believe that you deserve to be financially prosperous and successful, then the emotions that this creates can include fear, resistance, frustration, or anger.

The reverse is also true: when you believe that abundance is your natural state, you will experience feelings of joy, flow, and ease regarding money.

Changing Your Emotions Changes Your Beliefs

We just discussed that when you change your beliefs, you can change your corresponding emotion(s). It also works in the reverse. If you change the emotion, you can also change the belief. And as we know about the power of manifesting, your resulting experiences will be what you really believe to be true.

As such, it is important to pay attention to your emotions as a way to connect with your inner money reality. This is because your feelings regarding money are a reflection of your relationship with money, and ultimately, a reflection of your relationship with yourself.

Since money is emotional currency for women, it is

deeply personal and tied to our sense of self-worth and self-confidence and our sense of safety and security. One reason for this is that money serves as a stand-in for something else that we really want — love, security, identity, respect, or self-worth.

Given our discussions about the Law of Attraction and the power of our mind-set and emotions regarding money, whatever your deeper inner feelings are about money will eventually be reflected in your external experiences.

Your Emotions Cloud Your Financial Decisions

Your emotions have the power to dominate your behavior and decisions. To demonstrate this point, I would like to share an interesting metaphor — about the elephant and the rider, as introduced by psychologist Jonathan Haidt in his book *The Happiness Hypothesis*. The human mind has a rational side and an emotional side, resulting in two sometimes opposing forces that affect our emotions and behavior. The elephant represents our emotional side, governed by the reptilian part of the brain, which controls our basic impulses, fear and survival; and the brain's limbic system, which encircles the reptilian brain, controls our emotions and memories, and regulates behavior. The rider represents our rational side: the neocortex, the part of the brain that controls the logical, analytical, and reasoning aspects of the mind. When the elephant is trained well, it works in sync with the rider. However, when the elephant is not trained well, all logic can go out the window.

With regard to money, it can be especially difficult for the rider to control the elephant. The elephant can rule, given that the brain's reptilian side can completely override the neocortex. The chemicals in our emotional mind essentially hijack the rational mind, as though we were in life-threatening danger. Spending is primarily an emotional decision: when our feelings rule our actions, we spend impulsively. Thoughts of regret surface only afterward, which explains the scenarios of incurring high debt and credit card spending.

A major challenge to healing emotions regarding money is that many of us have learned poor coping skills when it comes to money, often stemming from our cultural and societal conditioning. Often we block our negative emotions by denying their existence, by pushing them aside, or by trying to ignore them altogether. Of course, these avoidance techniques only work for a period of time.

So why do we have poor coping skills when addressing negative emotions? We have learned that our feelings can create problems, so naturally we try to sidestep them. Ironically, problems arise not because we have these feelings but because we pay no attention to them. But ignoring hard feelings does not make them go away. In fact, this challenging cycle will continue to play an active role in your life — especially when it comes to your money.

Unlocking Your Emotions

Over the years, I have found four common emotions that arise when it comes to money. These feelings do not exclusively exist in women, since men also experience them, but in a different way. When not addressed and processed properly, these emotions can contribute to having an unhealed inner money reality. They can cloud your financial judgments and take away your power over money. These four feelings are fear, guilt, shame, and anger.

Let us examine in more detail the key emotions that can hold you back from greater financial success, as well as learn from the experiences of some courageous women.

Fear

Fear is perhaps the most common emotion we have — not just about money but about changing and stretching beyond our comfort zone toward the unknown. The hesitation many women experience with money usually centers on not having enough or fearing that whatever they have will be taken away or that they will lose it all. These feelings are connected to doubt and vulnerability. If you were exposed to this type of money anxiety while you were growing up, it can continue to resonate with you and has likely led you to re-create money drama in your life.

One common scenario is being afraid that you won't be able to pay the bills because there is not enough money. However, this fear can go much deeper. For example, many women fear becoming "bag ladies." In fact, nearly half of all women in the United States fear this — including those in households earning more than $200,000 a year — according to the 2013 Women, Money, and Power Study.

This statistic is a good example of how fear can control women. We women can be terrific worriers, even about events that are unlikely to happen. The fear of becoming a bag lady focuses on not being able to provide for yourself or your family, losing everything you have (including your ability to make a living), having someone take your money, or losing it all and becoming homeless. The fear also includes getting trapped in the cycle of dependency on other individuals or the government. What this really represents is a sense of being powerless and unable to survive.

I could go on providing examples of fear caused by the perspective of lack. However, there is also the fear of money caused by the perspective of abundance. I am referring to the fear of working really hard, becoming successful, and still losing it all. There is also the fear of experiencing so much success that the thought of embarking on a new project can cause anxiety for fear of failure, fear of judgment, and fear of losing success. Women who have these fears are often perfectionists. For example, women often sabotage themselves when negotiating their business contracts or salary by asking for less because they secretly fear that they can never live up to the level of success associated with the higher fee or salary. The fear of failure can plague female professionals who have already experienced a high level of success before heading into the next chapter.

I have personally experienced this, and so have other high-achieving women with whom I work. The good news is that we have the power to work through the fear and to experience freedom on the other side.

Feeling fearful about money can be distressing and consuming. Yet this distress acts as a powerful way to get your attention, reminding you of the importance of healing any unexamined fears related to money. Fear plays a critical role in signaling that you need to find the answers from deep within. This process can also help you to uncover your inner resources as well as to seek support and move forward.

SAMANTHA'S STORY

As I listened to Samantha, a brilliant social media expert, it was evident that she was at the end of her rope. Everyone she came into contact with believed she was exceptional, but the trouble was that Samantha herself did not believe it.

In fact, her self-confidence was at an all-time low. Before she started working with me, she was stuck at the same income level, no matter what she did. When we first met, she had just submitted her résumé for a "J.O.B." out of frustration and was convinced that after three years she was not meant to be an entrepreneur. She thought she did not have what it takes to be successful on her own.

The first thing I observed was that she was over-qualified for the position she was applying for, and the second thing I observed was that the salary would not comfortably support her and her family.

Samantha worried every day about paying the bills and feared that the heating in their house would be cut off, leaving her and her family to freeze in the middle of winter. Although her husband actually made a good salary and could provide for the family, Samantha was anxious that it was not enough. Fear and doubt had definitely camped out in her mind to the point where Samantha was stuck and simply had no momentum in her business.

She was in tears and mad at herself for having to give up her entrepreneurial dream. The sole glimmer of hope was that Samantha had decided to reach out for help because she truly wanted to change her story. Samantha had not really thought about her relationship with money before we began working together. However, according to her, she had tried everything else, so why not this? As we began our transformative work, she said in a voice that was barely a whisper, "You are my last hope."

Through our work, Samantha addressed her fears and emotions and finally healed her relationship with money. She never did take that job. Instead, she landed a lucrative multi-six-figure contract with a leading hotel chain to create and implement their marketing platform and social media strategy.

Guilt

Many women can identify with the emotion of guilt, especially when it comes to money. Guilty spending is a common money habit for women. You can recognize it when you find yourself telling others:

"I feel guilty whenever I'm spending instead of saving."

"I rarely buy anything unless it's on sale."

"I feel stressed out whenever I go over my budget."

Guilt as related to money usually stems from old fears and messages from childhood and is usually tied to not having had enough.

There is another side to guilt. It is in our nature as women to be nurturers, even to the point of martyrdom. This can show up in your willingness to spend and buy for others instead of yourself. This guilt can even lead you to give away money and lend money to family and friends, even when you know it will not be returned. This type of guilt leads to many women feeling more comfortable with giving than receiving and with being viewed as selfless.

The emotion of guilt can also be experienced by women who have become very wealthy. They feel guilty for having more money than their family or friends, so they may downplay their wealth or success.

Sofia is a wealthy, sophisticated, accomplished former executive. She lives in a beautiful home. Eight years ago she married a wealthy businessman. Instantly, her world became ultra-luxurious. The trouble is, she still identifies with her humble origins. It has taken her some time to adjust to her new social circles.

Sofia's story is inspiring. She escaped an abusive marriage with her two children and put herself through university part-time. Sofia went on to successfully climb the corporate ladder in a male-dominated industry.

At one point, before she left the corporate world, she was the vice president of an international company. This was after she married her second husband. Sofia started her own interior design company after leaving her corporate career, and although she no longer needs to rely on a salary, she does it because she loves being creative and making her own money.

She now has all the material wealth she ever could have imagined, yet Sofia feels guilty that financially, she and her siblings live in two very different worlds.

To compensate for this, Sofia preserves her "humble lifestyle" by shopping at thrift shops, not wearing expensive jewelry, and traveling economy class. In many ways, this behavior is her way of not "showing off" to her family. The curious part is that her family is very happy for her. We explored her underlying guilt and her beliefs about money so she could release them, once and for all, and instead leverage her business and status for social change.

Through our work, Sofia has accepted her newfound wealth and abundance with more gratitude. She has shifted her thoughts and emotions regarding money to match her lifestyle, and is now leveraging her wealth through soul-fulfilling philanthropic endeavors.

Shame

Of all the emotions regarding money, shame is perhaps the most difficult to endure. The emotion of shame cuts very deep to the core of who you are. It is based on the concept of not being "good enough," of being less than others, of having low self-worth, and of not deserving what you have. It points to being inadequate or flawed in some way.

As author Brené Brown notes, shame is "basically the fear of being unlovable." We have all experienced shame because it is a primal and universal human emotion. Yet many of us are afraid to talk about it, and because of this, it can continue to control our lives. Feelings of humiliation, embarrassment, and being judged by others can often surface, as well as guilt and anger. Shame is commonly experienced by those who amass a lot of debt and hide it, as we will see from the story below.

LINDA'S STORY

Linda is a lawyer who wants to transition from the corporate world into having her own practice. The trouble is, she has a habit of creating money drama.

During our first session she admitted to having amassed a high amount of debt from student loans, losing money on the equity of her home when she divorced her husband, and overspending on credit cards. Linda's total debt was close to the six-figure mark.

Although she was working with a financial advisor, Linda was carrying a lot of shame — so much so that she was hiding her mounting debts from family and friends. In fact, she censored what she said about her life and her financial travails. Linda was simply too embarrassed and did not want to be judged for having a life that was, in her own words, "out of control."

There was light at the end of the tunnel, since she was following a financial plan to address her debt. However, her sense of self-worth and confidence was lacking because the feelings of shame were so deep. Before we could work on putting her entrepreneurial plan into action, we had to first heal her relationship with money and with herself.

Our work together included releasing her feelings of shame and resentment left over from the divorce settlement. While this was not easy at first, Linda began to fill her cup with gratitude and self-love. Linda's break-through came when she began to dig deep and go within for answers. Then she took action by practicing self-love by being kind, gentle, and appreciative of herself. As she made progress, Linda began to trust herself again and to feel a sense of emotional harmony with her actions with money. She moved forward with greater self-confidence and self-worth.

Anger

The emotion of anger regarding money can leave you closed off emotionally and physically from others. It can keep the situation that you are angry about fresh in your mind, body, and spirit. The anger can also lead to blam-ing others for your challenging situation. In effect, anger and blame turn away money, opportunities, and people. The emotion of anger regarding money is based on be-lieving in the unfairness of life and/or the unfairness of money. The resulting blame is another way of directing anger at yourself or others.

If this is the case for you, perhaps you are angry at yourself for how you have handled your money. Perhaps you are angry at yourself, or someone else, for missing a great opportunity. Perhaps you blame your parents for letting you down in regard to money when you were growing up. Or maybe you blame your spouse or partner for letting you down with money. Most of all, maybe you are angry at having to start over again after having made poor money decisions. Anger and blame can lead to trust issues and believing that every cent of your money has to be protected because others might take advantage of you. They can even result in hoarding. Most of all, they can lead to feeling deprived in some way, prevented from attaining what you really want.

CHRISTINE'S STORY

Christine is a hospital administrator at one of the largest hospitals in the country. By her own admission, she is a workaholic. She is proud of herself for doing well in her career and for putting herself through undergraduate and graduate school by working two jobs. Christine still blames her parents (mostly her father) for disappointing her because they were irresponsible with their money and made some bad investments, leaving her with no money to pursue a higher education.

Christine is committed to her job and has accepted her status as a single woman; she just cannot seem to stay in a relationship for very long.

She is very careful with her money and likes to watch her bank accounts and investments increase. She admits that she does not like to part with money and that she rarely travels for vacation. Lately, she has been passed up for promotions at work, which she finds upsetting. She feels the company she works for takes her for granted, even though she works long hours and is very committed.

Christine came to me because she wanted to explore her emotions regarding money and whether these emotions were contributing to her being passed over for promotions. Through our work, Christine realized that her anger toward her parents and the company were misplaced. She was really angry at herself. Her anger was the barrier not only to getting a promotion but also to the rest of her life. In fact, she felt isolated in her world — no vacations, no deeper connections and friendships, and no joy. Perhaps the greatest lesson from this setback was that she needed to change course and start living fully.

One of Christine's assignments was to find ways to bring joy and fun into her life. The first action she took was to spend her money and go on a vacation — physically from work and emotionally from her anger. She began to get connected again with her friends and her parents, and even to socialize with her work colleagues. To her delight, she also began to laugh and smile more. Over a few months, her energy became lighter as she found ways to be true to herself.

Christine did get a promotion at another hospital seemingly out of the blue, helped along by a friend's referral. She credits her new and happier outlook to working on releasing her anger, which paved the way to more meaning and joy in her life.

The stories shared above point to the importance of understanding your underlying feelings as well as your unconscious motivations and beliefs regarding money. In essence, these negative attitudes generate inner conflicts. Internal obstacles are generally harder to recognize than external ones because with external obstacles the results are tangible, such as lack of income growth, lack of opportunities, and so forth. However, your underlying emotions can contribute significantly to the results that you experience in your work and life.

Some Self-Sabotaging Actions

Based on the stories and examples above, let us now examine four major ways in which women engage in self-sabotage: underearning, undercharging, undervaluing, and unclear boundaries. These actions are guided by your beliefs, habits, attitudes, and emotions, and by your relationship with money. If these issues are left unexamined, money problems will persist, thereby keeping you from experiencing the joy, wealth, satisfaction, and success you desire.

Underearning

I have known many women trapped in the category of underearner — and it is seldom a conscious choice. Essentially, you are an underearner when your income is not reflective of your skills, talents, and potential, despite your efforts. You are also underearning when, even though you work very hard, logging long hours, you know you are not earning what you deserve for the value you provide. This can leave you feeling less confident, frustrated, and stuck. It can also cause you to give away your power by blaming others or external factors for your situation.

SARAH'S STORY

Sarah is a sought-after psychic and has been featured on television and radio shows and in magazines. She loves helping people create breakthroughs in their lives. Her schedule is always full, and she has a waiting list. She has started to work internationally and has many overseas clients.

After being referred by a friend, Sarah came to see me to get to the bottom of her emotions about money, particularly her feeling that money is not important. In many respects she fit the classic description of the heart-centered nurturer who says, "It's not about the money. I just want to help people."

Upon assessing her business, we saw she was charging too little, had a limited way of accepting payments, had no accountant or bookkeeper, and on it went.

It was evident that in order to move forward, Sarah first had to come to terms with the idea that she could be spiritual and make money at the same time. This also included the idea that her ability to help many more people means that she can also be rewarded for her value in helping others.

Our work together included helping Sarah to connect money with her spiritual purpose, which was very important to her. She was then able to believe that she could make great money while being spiritual at the same time. Sarah became more grateful and tracked examples of abundance in all areas of her life, especially in her work. She was very pleasantly surprised to find that she could achieve her bold money goal in a short amount of time.

Undercharging

Another action that can limit financial prosperity is the practice of undercharging, which is similar to underearning. Many women tend to overdeliver and undercharge. Do you find yourself wanting to nurture and care for everyone and also secretly wanting to be liked by everyone? If so, you are not alone. Many women want to please everyone, even at their own expense. This pattern can become a normal way of doing business, even when deep inside, you may resent it. With this self-sabotaging pattern of trying to buy approval, you can become self-critical and start to blame yourself.

JILLIAN'S STORY

Jillian is a psychotherapist specializing in couple's and family counseling. She is well known in her community and has a reputation for being great at what she does. She loves her work, but when she came to see me, Jillian was frustrated because she was not earning enough money. Every month she would just break even after expenses, which left her feeling stressed and resentful. She often compared herself to her other female colleagues who were getting paid well for doing what they loved. They would go on vacations; they had savings and investments; overall, they had a good quality of life.

Through our work, Jillian recognized that her inability to say no to her clients and the fact that she had charged the same fee for the past five years were forms of self-sabotage. In particular, Jillian realized that she was overdelivering in her sessions by being too accessible without charging for it. She also feared discussing money and raising her fees with her clients. In effect, she was not honoring her own value.

Through our work together, she strengthened her trust in herself and her talents. We practiced having money conversations with her clients, particularly when discussing her fees.

As our sessions moved forward, Jillian was gaining more self-confidence and courage. She finally made the bold move to raise her fees and restructure her services. To her joy, her clients were more than willing to pay her new rates without hesitation, pleasantly saying, "Okay." The bonus is that she got on the path to a thriving six-figure income.

Undervaluing

The third major action that prevents women from generating greater financial prosperity is the habit of undervaluing themselves and their time. Here are some common examples that indicate that you may be undervaluing yourself and the products, services, or work you provide. These include but are not limited to:

- undervaluing your time and giving it away for free
- discounting your prices when people request it
- discounting your prices even when people do not request it, and secretly resenting it
- overworking and doing everything yourself, then feeling overwhelmed and exhausted

A vital way to honor your value is to offer your work only to those who value it because they are more likely to benefit, to use it for their highest good, and in turn, to help others, creating a positive domino effect.

ANGIE'S STORY

Angie is a photographer specializing in weddings and other events. To stay competitive, she consistently undercuts her prices but secretly harbors some resentment because she often works long hours, especially on weekends, leaving little time for a social life. Yet when others have suggested that she add to her team, Angie has resisted.

Deep within herself, Angie is afraid to give up control, especially when it comes to her profits.

Our work involved helping Angie realize that she had an opportunity to create a win-win situation in that the value she provided to everyone else could also come back to her. That is, she was part of the full circle of value and abundance. She acknowledged that she was busy giving, but not receiving, so there was an imbalance in her work and life. This brought on feelings of resentment and distrust.

Angie began to learn how to value herself first before she could add value to others. She decided to fill her cup through self-care, replenishing her energy and spirit. Then she released resistance to hiring qualified team members whom she can trust and rely on. In the end, Angie found the value she was seeking, had more time for a social life, and saw her profits grow. Finally, she had achieved balance in her life.

Unclear Boundaries

The fourth major action that limits women's prosperity and success is having unclear personal boundaries. I define personal boundaries as having rules, guidelines, and limits as to what is permissible in how others behave toward you. Your boundary defines who you are as an individual. Having well-developed personal boundaries is key to having satisfying relationships and self-confidence.

Often, it is difficult to recognize this dynamic, making it a major blind spot for women regarding their money. Having unclear boundaries can show up for you in the following ways:

- Clients not paying on time
- Clients dropping out of your program(s)
- Consistently going over time (for service-based businesses)
- Consistently being relied on to work overtime in your job
- Attracting clients, customers, or colleagues who are demanding and high-maintenance
- Saying yes when you really mean no in all areas of your life, including with money
- Experiencing difficulties regarding money conversations with clients, partners, banks, financial professionals, your spouse, or family members
- Failing to be completely clear regarding your policies, often skipping these discussions with new clients

JENNIFER'S STORY

Jennifer loves being a coach because she gets to help people transform their lives. She often provides coaching to friends and colleagues for free. However, Jennifer secretly has started to resent the arrangement, but she fears discussing the matter with those participating.

When we began working together, it became clear that she was struggling with asserting her boundaries, even with her clients. Jennifer was giving away her time for free. Her twenty-minute "right-fit" call would turn out to actually take forty-five minutes, and she would do some coaching during the phone call as well.

It did not take Jennifer long to make the connection that, for her, the "hook" was that she wanted to be liked. She also had the "disease to please," just as she had had when she was a child. However, now it was costing her time, energy, and money in her business. Jennifer realized she was enabling her clients and friends to continue this pattern because she herself was not valuing her time, boundaries, and expertise.

We immediately got to work, helping her shift her mind-set and habits, strengthening her boundaries, and taking actions with money that honored her. The combination of working on her mind-set, boundaries, and actions was what she needed to feel empowered — with herself and her relationship with money. As a result, she learned how to say no by tightening her boundaries, thereby releasing her need to please. Jennifer became more empowered in all other areas of her life.

Making Lemonade

Did you recognize elements of your relationship with money in any of the examples and stories above? Did any of the key emotions surface for you?

If you recognized yourself in these stories and identified with the emotions of fear, guilt, shame, or anger, take heart, because you are definitely not alone. At some point in our lives, we have all felt these emotions. And this is actually a good thing because you can now face them with courage and grace. It is also normal that you may even feel a sense of failure about some of your choices and actions with money.

I truly believe that there are benefits to failure. I am not glorifying the experience of failure, since having been there myself, I know how painful it can be. However, I do believe that in moments of failure, a seed of learning and insight has been planted that can, if we are willing to pay attention to the lesson, lead us to a feeling of freedom. This insight can also lead us to take action, despite our fear of failure.

One of the best descriptions of the benefits of failure that I have come across is from J. K. Rowling, who gave a commencement speech at Harvard University. In her speech she described her experience of failure and rebuilding her life. Here is a brief excerpt:

> Ultimately, we all have to decide for ourselves what constitutes failure, but the world is quite eager to give you a set of criteria if you let it. So I think it fair to say that by any conventional measure, a mere seven years after my graduation day, I had failed on an epic scale. An exceptionally short-lived marriage

had imploded, and I was jobless, a lone parent, and as poor as it is possible to be in modern Britain without being homeless. The fears that my parents had had for me, and that I had had for myself, had both come to pass, and by every usual standard, I was the biggest failure I knew....

So why do I talk about the benefits of failure? Simply because failure meant a stripping away of the inessential. I stopped pretending to myself that I was anything other than what I was, and began to direct all my energy into finishing the only work that mattered to me. Had I really succeeded at anything else, I might never have found the determination to succeed in the one arena I believed I truly belonged. I was set free because my greatest fear had been realised, and I was still alive, and I still had a daughter whom I adored, and I had an old typewriter and a big idea. And so rock bottom became the solid foundation on which I rebuilt my life.

Moving Past the Emotions
That Stand between You and Prosperity

With my clients I often share a powerful ten-step exercise that focuses on forgiveness and letting go of what no longer serves you. (You can download the exercise at the end of this chapter.)

While this may not seem relevant to money, it actually is because the act of forgiveness will truly set you free.

And this feeling of freedom will enable you to release any related or lingering negative emotions of anger, fear, worry, and the like. The act provides you with an opportunity to forgive the past and the people who have shaped your beliefs, habits, and attitude regarding money. More important, it provides you with an opportunity to forgive yourself for the actions you have or have not taken with money.

To help you get started, open your journal and answer the following four questions that focus primarily on the emotion of anger:

1. Is there anyone in your current life or your past (including yourself) with whom you are angry regarding money?
2. What are you specifically angry about?
3. How has this anger impacted the flow of abundance in your life?
4. Are you now willing to forgive?

Forgiving is extremely hard for many people to embrace. You may not be ready for it to happen all at once. It may need to happen as a process over time. Either way, forgiving is a vital aspect of healing your relationship with money.

Remember, forgiving is not something you do for the sake of others. Forgiveness is something you do for yourself as part of an "emotional decluttering." What you are really doing is focusing your energy on more positive pursuits and making space for the good that you desire.

Exercise: Releasing Emotional Blocks to Wealth

This is another helpful exercise I have created, and it can help you shift your emotions of fear, guilt, shame, and anger regarding money so you can break free of the emotional blocks preventing you from enjoying prosperity. The five steps are:

Step 1. Open to a blank page in your journal and draw four columns. The title of the first column is "Fear"; the title of the second column is "Whose Fear Is It?"; the title of the third column is "Behavior"; and the title of the fourth column is "Truth."

Step 2. In the first column, list all the fears you are aware that you have regarding money. Keep in mind that sometimes fears disguise themselves. For example, going without and not spending, even when you really need to spend on something, is a sure sign of fear. Be really honest with yourself here.

Step 3. In the second column, identify the origin of this fear, often childhood experiences and traumas.

Step 4. In the third column, identify the behavior this fear translates into, for example, hoarding and not parting with belongings.

Step 5. In the fourth column, list a new belief that you want as your truth, for example, "I generate money to meet all my needs."

Repeat this exercise for the emotions of guilt, shame, and anger.

CHAPTER SUMMARY

- The four common emotional triggers that arise over money are fear, guilt, shame, and anger. These emotions contribute to having an unhealed inner money reality and can prevent money from flowing freely into your life.

- You express your emotions through your financial decisions and actions, which helps to explain your current pattern with money.

- Your current income represents your past, not your future. Your ability to break through and let go of disempowering beliefs, habits, and actions regarding money goes a long way toward recognizing that these emotions are no longer serving who you are and the success you desire.

- Addressing your emotional blocks to wealth includes facing and healing your negative feelings regarding money. It also includes understanding the underlying causes of your emotions and problem-solving ways to prevent them from becoming obstacles to achieving your financial goals.

• A key way to move past your emotional blocks with money is to let them go and to forgive yourself and others. Practicing forgiveness is a powerful way to remove whatever is standing between you and having more money in your life.

Take Action

Bonus download at:
www.MoneyManifestationAndMiracles.com/gift

Ten Steps to Forgiveness Exercise

Chapter 10

Holistic Principle 4

CONFIDENTLY EXPRESS YOURSELF

Rich thoughts, rich words, rich actions, rich offerings.
With those elements in place you are living a rich life indeed.
— SUZE ORMAN

As you are discovering on this journey, money is a mysterious force. On the one hand, it is a powerful tool because we can do remarkable things with it. Money can be a tremendous force for good, an agent for change and transformation, and an expression of love. Money can make our lives easier, alleviate problems, help us achieve health and happiness, and enable us to contribute to humanity's betterment. On the other hand, even in our age of advanced technology, scientific achievements, and well-educated, intelligent citizens, money remains somewhat of a secret and a mystery.

Money is an uncomfortable topic for many people.

We are more comfortable talking about our deepest fears or the intimacies of our personal lives than we are talking about how much we earn, how much debt we have, or how much is in our bank account. It just feels too personal. Often our conversations about money stay at a practical and transactional level rather than at a deeper heart-and-soul level.

Talking about money is still a cultural taboo, especially in social situations. In fact, I can almost guarantee your exclusion from future party invitations if you were to ask your hosts and guests how much money they make. It would be considered inappropriate and impolite. This is because, as you know, money is rarely just about money. Discussions about money trigger strongly held beliefs and emotions within you and all of us. Of course, your words are really an extension of your thoughts, beliefs, and emotions. Thus, we keep our words to ourselves so as not to expose too much.

In this chapter, our focus is on the holistic principle of expression and helping you communicate about money in a more positive and optimistic way. This will enhance the quality of your conversations regarding money with clients, partners, family, friends, colleagues, and more. It will also enhance the quality of your internal monologue.

Whether or not you are conscious of it, you are talking and communicating about money every day. What words do you use when talking about money? Is your vocabulary primarily positive and empowering or negative and disempowering?

Here's a Reality Check

If you were to take a step back and listen to yourself speak about your money, what would you hear? Would you hear phrases such as:

"I can't..."
"I will never have..."
"I wish I had..."
"I never will..."
"I really should..."

Would you prefer instead to hear words such as:

"I can..."
"I always have..."
"I am happy I have..."
"I am grateful for..."

I suggest that you start paying attention to what you say about your money. The result can be surprising. And if you do not like what you are hearing, simply change your approach.

The words you use to communicate about money to your clients, significant other, family, friends, colleagues, business partners, the bank, and others matter. If you are a business owner, the words you use with your clients and customers regarding money are critical to your success. You may not realize it, but your words contain tremendous power.

Words that are repeated often enough become true, because what you focus on grows. The way you express yourself about money contains a powerful energy. If you use statements such as:

"I never have enough money."
"I have a love/hate relationship with money."
"I'm not good with money."
"I'd rather not have to think about money."

and you repeat them often enough, your words are technically creating your reality, since these statements are a form of affirmations. So the goal is to be very mindful about how you express yourself when it comes to money. Choose words of wealth rather than scarcity. You are likely unaware of how powerful your words are and of their impact — not just on other people but also on you. Additionally, your overall style of communication influences your emotions. For example, if your style of communicating is calm and thoughtful, the energy is harmonious and not chaotic. However, if your style of self-expression is hurried, impatient, or anger based, the energy that it creates is drama, confrontation, negativity, and highly charged emotions.

Many women I work with experience challenges when having money conversations, particularly when it comes to stating their fees or salary and charging and getting paid their worth. As we've seen, at the root of this is their conflicting emotions about themselves and their worth. These feelings simply materialize in their words and actions. Many women can find themselves providing discounts or working overtime, since they think it will help them secure clients or get a promotion. These actions often lead to being overwhelmed and overworked and to blame, resentment, and low self-confidence.

DEBBIE'S STORY

Debbie is a nutritionist on a mission to empower people and communities through healthy eating, exercise, and lifestyle balance. When she was fourteen, her father died of a sudden heart attack. He was a workaholic executive who was overweight, smoked heavily, and ignored warnings from doctors, his wife, family, and friends. This tragedy motivated Debbie to seek a career in helping people embrace a healthy lifestyle.

While people are drawn to Debbie because of her expertise, energy, and personal story, she was still having a hard time earning more than $80,000, even though she works long hours and is highly committed to her mission. She knew this level of income would simply not allow her to reach more people or fulfill her mission. And that's what frustrated her.

As we began to dig deeper, it quickly became clear that Debbie felt a lot of fear when it came to discussing finances. She was raised in a family that did not talk about money. She only heard raised voices when her parents discussed this taboo topic, so she associated money with tension and anxiety.

Now this problem was affecting her when she spoke with potential and existing clients about her rates. She would state her fees for her service and packages, and when there was silence while people contemplated their decision, Debbie would become anxious. So she would often jump the gun by saying, "But I can give you a deal" and proceed to offer discounts, even if a discounted rate had not even been requested. And when others would come right out and ask for a better deal, she would readily agree, even though she secretly resented it.

Either way, her fear of avoiding talking about money was keeping Debbie from reaching more people and making a meaningful difference. Her breakthrough came when she separated the tragedy of her father's passing from the memories of family arguments over money. Though these were two discrete events, somehow she had linked the two in her mind. This was a freeing experience for Debbie. Once she fully integrated this understanding, we were able to address her resistance around money. Debbie has gone on to take greater interest in her finances and have money conversations with clients and others with more ease than she ever had before.

Words of Wealth

It is not enough to push away negative thoughts and words of lack or poverty. We must also use words of wealth and abundance more often. One way to shift your actions is to check in with yourself before you say something about your money. For example, you might frequently say:

"I will never get out of debt."

"My clients will not pay me that much money."

"I cannot ask for a raise."

"I can't charge that amount."

If you do, first ask yourself the question, "Is this the reality I want?" The answer, I am sure, is a resounding no!

The Power to Reframe Your Words

You have the power to choose to reframe your thoughts and words to create a more positive outcome. Here are some examples of reframes:

Limiting Words	Reframing the Words
"I will never get out of debt."	"In six months (choose a realistic time frame), I am going to be debt free."
"My clients won't pay me more."	"My clients happily pay me for helping and empowering them to achieve results."
"I cannot ask for a raise."	"I am valued for my expertise and contribution to the organization's success."

The key here is to take action to reframe. (You can download the reframe exercise at the end of this chapter.)

As you begin to change your thoughts and words, negative thoughts will still arise, which is normal. Just be aware of whenever you are expressing negative and limiting words. Then you can quickly interrupt yourself and replace those words with terms that express your true values regarding money. Choose positive words of abundance that convey the reality you want to experience.

A Bonus Tip

Remove the word *should* from your vocabulary. As the great Louise Hay once said, "*Should* is one of the most damaging words in our language. Every time we use it, we are, in effect, saying that we *are* wrong, or we *were* wrong....Replace *should* with *could*."

The Power of Affirmations

As you begin to take consistent action to reframe your words, the next step is to leverage the power of affirmations. As we discussed in chapter 5, many people use affirmations to bring about new conditions in their lives. To review, affirmations are positive statements that can help focus your awareness and energy on creating what you want. Essentially, they are about "affirming" what you want. To experience successful results with affirmations, use positive words and then put energy behind them by applying the four key ingredients:

1. Having a strong conviction that the affirmation is happening in the present moment
2. Feeling good about yourself and your circumstances in the present tense, which raises your personal energy
3. Taking action
4. Surrendering the outcome with trust, faith, and love while being ready to receive

This is where magic truly happens in transitioning from the unmanifested to the manifested.

As we've seen, in order for your affirmations to work in your favor, you must use only affirmations that:

- you truly believe in (even if it is a stretch and currently not your reality)
- feel appropriate for you and possible
- you believe are the truth (i.e., you can begin to "act as if")

Therefore, if you are saying affirmations that feel impossible to create, you will not get the results you want, since you will not be able to generate the energy, emotions, and trust required to create what you desire. For example:

Limiting Beliefs	Positive Affirmations
"I now have one million dollars" (yet deep down you do not believe it is possible, or your reality is that you can't pay the bills and you know it is "pie in the sky").	"I am grateful to now have ____" (include the amount that is exciting, is a stretch, and a money breakthrough for you, plus one you truly believe you can have).
"I cannot make more than I earned in the past or exceed my current level of success."	"As an expert business-woman and leader, there are no limits to my in-come."

Keep in mind that you can achieve this sum or any sum in the future when you truly believe. This action is part of stair-stepping your big leaps.

CHAPTER SUMMARY

- Money is an uncomfortable topic for many people. In most cases, it is still considered a cultural taboo to speak about money in social situations. We are more comfortable talking about our deepest fears and sharing the details of our private lives than we are talking about money, which just feels too personal.

- There is tremendous power in your words. They have the power to uplift or disempower others — and, more important, you.
- Your words are an extension of your thoughts. To change your words, you must first change your thoughts.
- Pay attention to the words you are using regarding money and all areas of your life. Through the power of manifesting, you create the reality that you believe to be true.
- Before saying anything about your money such as "I cannot get out of debt" or "I never have enough money," first ask yourself, "Is this the experience I want?"
- You have the power to reframe your statements into ones that empower you, such as "In six months (or whatever the time frame), I am going to be debt free."
- To master money and increase your financial prosperity, you must learn the language of wealth and abundance. This includes having wealthy thoughts, using words of wealth when speaking about money, and taking actions from the place of an empowered mind-set.
- For affirmations to work in your favor, you must use only those that feel most appropriate for you, as well as those that feel possible. If you are saying affirmations that feel impossible to create, you will not get the results you desire and will feel

frustrated. You can stair-step and stretch yourself beyond your comfort zone in order to make bigger leaps into the future.

- It is not enough to push away negative thoughts and words of lack or poverty to create your new reality. You must begin to speak positively about your money and use words of wealth, starting today. This action will profoundly impact the future you create.

Take Action

Bonus download at:
www.MoneyManifestationAndMiracles.com/gift

Reframe Exercise: transform limiting words into empowering thoughts, words, and actions.

Chapter 11

Holistic Principle 5

CREATE YOUR
LASTING IMPACT

*There is no passion to be found in playing small — in settling for
a life that is less than the one you are capable of living.*
— NELSON MANDELA

IN CHAPTER 7, we discussed the significance of being in
alignment with who you are and everything you do. You
completed various exercises to help you gain clarity of
your strengths and personal values.

In this chapter our focus is on the holistic principle
of purpose. We will build on what you've learned about
your strengths and values, and align them with your passion, purpose, and greater "why" with money — your
deeper reason for wanting to make more of it. This chapter will also help you to align with your social promise
and the impact you want to make on the world.

For many women, the answer to the question of "why"

as it pertains to making more money does not come easily. This is because, as we've seen, for most women the connection to money is not as straightforward as it is for men. For women the connection to money is more about relationships and meaning. The good news is that you can use this awareness to your advantage in generating your desired income and in fueling your vision and mission. Understanding your greater "why" with money can help you deepen and anchor your connection to money. Once you are aligned with your purpose and your "why," you will become even more inspired to do what you love while making a meaningful difference in the process.

Your Unique Fingerprint

Your life's purpose is unique to you, as singular as your fingerprint. Some refer to their life's purpose as their calling or even their destiny. Essentially, your life's purpose is the reason you are here. Since your life's purpose is about accomplishing what gives you meaning and fulfillment, it naturally affects you on other important levels of your existence:

Soul: Your whole heart and being are deeply connected to your purpose. As such, you must nurture, protect, and cherish it at all times.

Spiritual: As the French Jesuit priest Pierre Teilhard de Chardin once said: "We are not human beings having a spiritual experience. We are spiritual beings having a human experience." Spirituality is a broader concept than religion, although religion can be one expression of it. Other expressions of spirituality include prayer, meditation, spending time in nature, generosity to causes, and more. Essentially, spirituality is a deep, soulful connection to God — or however you choose to identify God: Divine Source, Higher Power, Source Energy, Spirit, or Infinite Intelligence. You are connected to Divine Source Energy at all times. Therefore, your life's purpose is also a manifestation of your spirituality.

Emotional: Since your life's purpose impacts your heart, soul, and spirit on a deeper level, your emotions and feelings are also naturally impacted. The main emotion that your life's purpose can bring you is love, including love for your purpose, love for your passion, and love for how you can affect others and the world.

Psychological: Your mind-set plays a major role in helping you nurture and accomplish your life's purpose. Having the right strategies and tools at hand will be a source of support for you. When you do encounter obstacles and experience limited states of mind, know that these represent only temporary clouds (your thoughts) that eclipse the sun (your true state of being).

Physical: Accomplishing your purpose on the physical level means taking consistent and intentional actions to make it a reality, since without action, the best plans will not bear fruit. Taking intentional actions also includes trusting your intuition, leveraging the various Universal

Laws and Spiritual Laws, and not letting opportunities pass you by.

We need to distinguish life purpose from vision and mission since the three are sometimes used interchangeably. Simply, your mission is the way you choose to fulfill your purpose, and your vision is a compelling image of the future.

Your life's purpose, however, is what Paulo Coelho calls your "Personal Legend." He describes it in his book *The Alchemist* as "what you have always wanted to accomplish. Everyone, when they are young, knows what their Personal Legend is. At that point in their lives, everything is clear and everything is possible. They are not afraid to dream, to yearn for everything they would like to see happen to them in their lives. But, as time passes, a mysterious force begins to convince them that it will be impossible for them to realize their Personal Legend."

As we grow older, it becomes easier to get disconnected from our authentic and innermost dreams of what we really wish to accomplish. Our fears and doubts begin to surface, as well as the fact that society, and even our family, does not always help us to nurture these dreams. As a result, we tend not to honor our dreams for fear of failure, fear of hearing those dreaded words "I told you so," or fear of getting it wrong. Often what happens is that people become resigned to what they think they "should" be and do, and they move forward in their lives by just existing. In other words, they settle, accepting less than what they originally sought and felt they truly deserved.

When I work with clients, I am amazed at how often they become tearful when they start reconnecting with their real purpose and dust off their innermost dreams. The truth is that life happens, and we simply do not take the time to check in with ourselves and nurture what really brings us joy, meaning, and fulfillment.

As for myself, my life's purpose did not automatically surface for me, and it did take some soul-searching to reconnect with it. As I shared earlier, my life's purpose is to understand and create wealth — in all its forms — and to help others do the same. As my path unfolded, I realized a more meaningful way to express my purpose by empowering women to claim their wealth and to thrive — living lives of purpose, wealth, and significance while being a force of good in the world.

Let me ask you this:

- What is your life's purpose?
- Are you living it?
- What gives you fulfillment and meaning?
- How are you expressing your life's purpose through your life's work?

Each of us has a wonderful opportunity to express our passions and achieve our goals and dreams through our life's work. In fact, when you are aligned with your purpose, your work becomes an expression of your passions and of the contribution that you want to make to the world.

The three best ways to discover your purpose and align it with your life's work are, first, tapping into your passion, because your passion leaves clues as to what really fulfills you; second, reconnecting with your greater "why" and purpose with money, which will act as a motivator for why you are doing what you are doing; and third, creating your purpose and impact statement. Let's talk about these three techniques in greater detail.

Fuel Your Passion

The first and most important way to discover your life's purpose is to connect with your passion. Many people may confuse searching for their passion with an external pursuit. The truth is that your passion is already within you at this very moment. Your passion already provides you with a source of enthusiasm, energy, and focus in any activity you are drawn to. And when you can express your passion through your life's work, you are better able to get into alignment with the energy and flow of attracting abundance into your life.

Here I want to share a fun exercise that I created called the Passion Treasure Quest, which will help you tap into your passion by providing clues about what awakens your enthusiasm, as identified in everyday situations. (You can download the complete exercise at the end of the chapter). In the same way that success leaves a footprint, so does your passion. This exercise will help you discover it.

To go on your passion quest, please answer the following questions:

- What do you love to do that makes you feel *alive*?
- What were you passionate about as a child? Why?
- What have you always secretly wanted to do but were held back from doing by fear, doubt, a lack of confidence, and so on?
- Whose life would you love to have? Why?
- What do your ideal life and work look like?

Reconnect with Your Greater "Why" and Align It with Money

The second way to align your purpose with your life's work is to reconnect with your greater "why." By this I mean gaining clarity as to why you are doing what you are doing, and how you can align it with money in order to experience greater fulfillment.

Moving beyond generating income, ask yourself these questions:

- Why does your business exist? Or why did you choose this specific career or job?
- What makes it right for you?
- Why do you use your precious energy and time to do what you do?
- What is the driving force behind what you do?

Many women I work with have experienced a high level of success through their former corporate roles. So when they decided to strike out on their own, they often had a bigger "why" that pulled them forward. Deep within there was a strong pull for them to accomplish their goals, while also being richly rewarded for doing what they love and making a meaningful impact.

NICOLE'S STORY

Nicole is a journalist and former executive in the television news industry. When the network downsized, she was let go and found herself at a crossroads.

At forty-two, Nicole knew she could start a brand-new career if she wanted. She was grateful for having received a generous severance package, which if she was careful with it, could last two years while she pondered what she wanted to do next. She knew for sure that another executive position was not what she was looking for. She felt that it was time for her to reconnect with her dreams.

When we began working together, Nicole shared that she missed traveling and covering inspirational stories that motivated and uplifted people and that she wanted to do that instead of covering the latest disasters and scandals to score TV ratings. She got into journalism in the first place because of her childhood dream of writing and traveling. Over the years she had lost that connection.

Nicole reconnected with her dreams and rediscovered that she really wanted to share messages of inspiration and hope with people around the world, especially with women in developing countries. Through our work, she decided to start her own documentary film company and took advantage of all the contacts she had made from years of working in the television and media industry. She also leveraged her contacts in large corporations that support finding solutions for social issues. The documentaries Nicole went on to produce focus on inspirational people from around the world who overcome adversities and make a difference in their communities.

Nicole was living her dream on her own terms, combining her life's work and income with her passion and purpose.

Included in this step is aligning your greater "why" with money. This will help you to anchor what it means to experience prosperity and fulfillment. It will also provide you with clarity about the amount you want to generate and for what purpose. It is essential to understand what motivates you to generate this income.

Ask yourself:

- What is the money for?
- Why do I want this amount?
- What purpose will it serve?
- Why is it meaningful to me?

Once you have clarity on your money goal and the purpose behind that goal, this clarity will fuel your motivation, especially in times of frustration and doubt, and will help move you toward your vision.

Using your journal, complete the exercise below to help you further align with your money "why."

Exercise: Harmonizing Your Greater "Why" with Money

Please complete the sentence below:

My big money goal is to make _____ (amount) by _____ (date), so that I can _____ (your "why").

This is important to me because _____ _____.

Remind yourself often of your purpose and mission by reviewing this exercise daily.

State Your Purpose and Impact

The third way to align with your purpose is to create a purpose and impact statement. This is similar to having a memento or reminder that you can use as a reference point to keep you focused.

Your purpose statement is personal to you. It can be

as splendid and bold as you want it to be. You can share it with others, incorporate it into your business vision or personal mission, or simply keep it to yourself. Whatever you decide to do, it can be helpful to also include a larger impact statement that goes beyond you, describing how you would like to affect others personally and profession-ally through your work.

There are many ways to approach developing your purpose and impact statement. The exercise below is just one way. Feel free to create your own process (see the ex-amples below).

Exercise: Purpose and Impact Statement

Draft your purpose statement in your journal:

My purpose is to _____

_____ so that

_____

_____ (outcome).

Here are some examples of purpose and impact state-ments that some of my clients have developed:

- My purpose is to be a catalyst so that people are motivated to make positive changes in their lives.
- My purpose is to live joyfully by helping others

so they can direct their challenges into sources of learning and growth.

- My purpose is to lead organizations in a positive way so that others are inspired to contribute meaningfully.
- My purpose is to inspire others so they can achieve their dreams (shorter version).

A Bonus Tip

First and foremost, you must feel drawn to your purpose and impact statement. It must stir excitement, and you must feel passionate about it. Here are some guidelines for developing your statement. Your statement must:

- have a strong emotional connection with your purpose.
- ring true for you.
- feel joyful and exciting.
- motivate and inspire you to act on it.

Creating Your Ripple Effect

What lasting impact or legacy do you want to create through your life's work?

Since for women money is about relationships, meaning, connections, and sharing, once their needs and their families' needs are met, most women use their money to help others and contribute to making the world a better place. In fact, on average women reinvest 90 cents of every dollar they earn to family education, health, and nutrition. This is why aligning social promise and impact is a natural fit for women. This is especially the case for business owners and leaders, who have the power to leverage their business and income to fuel a broader social mission.

As noted, social promise is your soul's desire to give back by doing good while doing well in life. It includes a dual goal of combining wealth and profits with a mission to better society. Fulfilling your social promise can be expressed in many ways, such as supporting worthy local or global causes and issues you most care about.

The phenomenon of organizations creating positive social change is not new. In fact, the concept of corporate social responsibility has existed since at least the 1960s. However, bringing change to communities and the world has become more mainstream in the past decade, as large corporations and nonprofit organizations have become involved in the movement. A great example of this is the "conscious capitalism" movement created by John Mackey, cofounder and CEO of Whole Foods Market. Conscious capitalism is basically about balancing business profits with social impact.

Your social promise can motivate you to align your purpose and passion with service and contribution. Likewise, your contributions to others as a result of your professional endeavors will allow you to change lives while also deeply enriching your own life — and your bottom line — beyond your fondest dreams. And this is what being in full alignment can look like for you, living your purpose through your life's work and achieving financial prosperity while making a meaningful difference in the world.

Myths and Truths about Social Promise

When many people think about making a social impact, they do not think that this change can extend to themselves and their life's work. On the one hand, it feels exciting and worthwhile to take on a worthy cause, and on the other, it can feel too time consuming and overwhelming. Below I debunk many of the myths that exist about expressing one's social promise through one's life's work, and reaping the financial rewards of doing so.

Social Promise Myth 1. Making a social impact is only for big corporations.

Truth: Actually, creating a change and making a social impact is suitable for all businesses, including small ones. In fact, creating social change has real business and economic value. Many consumers support businesses that have strong principles and stand for something such as improving the environment and going "green," as well as only buying organic products, and so forth. This approach can put your business on the map and generate loyal clients and customers.

Social Promise Myth 2. Having a social promise is only for businesses and companies that are already generating big profits.

Truth: This is not strictly the case. You can incorporate your social promise into your company's mission statement right from the start. You can also earmark certain projects to fund your social promise. This is a fun and creative way to start making an impact right away.

Using my business as an example, a portion of the proceeds of the sale of this book will go to organizations that support women's economic empowerment. Just think, your purchasing this book is helping another woman create a better life for herself and her family.

When you are involved in these types of activities through your work, you are also activating the Universal Law of Giving and Receiving (see chapter 5).

Social Promise Myth 3. I will develop my social promise when I'm ready to create my legacy.

Truth: This is a common mind-set among many women, who feel they are "not successful enough" or "not ready yet."

You can start creating your legacy right now in your business or career. Your legacy is not just what you do; it is who you are and the significant gifts you want to bestow on the world. You do not have to wait until all the conditions are perfect. Granted, creating a legacy is a longer-term goal; however, you have the power now to share your message of how you want to make the world a better place. Every step you take builds on your legacy.

Social Promise Myth 4. This is not for me. My business does not have a social focus. Or, this is not for me because I do not own a business.

Truth: This is another common mind-set. However, even if you are not conscious of it, as an ambitious and heart-centered woman, you cannot help but make an impact with your work. This is because your life's work is in full alignment with who you are, what matters most to you, your purpose, and the difference you want to make.

Additionally, even if you are not a business owner, you can apply the concept of *tithing* — giving and donating 10 percent of your income — as a way of making a difference in the world. (While 10 percent is recommended, the exact percentage is a personal decision based on your situation.) As we saw in chapter 5, the act of tithing is a powerful spiritual practice and part of the Universal and Spiritual Laws of Giving and Receiving.

Many of my clients who did not initially believe they had a social promise were surprised to find that they did. They discovered that through their life's work, they were actually starting a movement or taking a stand on something they were passionate about.

KATE'S STORY

Kate has a PhD in social work and is a former researcher and college professor. She is now an author and consultant focusing on helping women executives and leaders take on CEO and presidential roles in large corporations.

Kate was amazed to find that a lack of self-confidence was still very much a contributing factor in preventing women from advancing in their fields. When we began working together to broaden her revenue streams, Kate also reconnected with her values, purpose, and passion. She did not realize it at first, but what she really wanted to do was to create a movement to boost the self-esteem of young girls, starting at the age of ten, of teenagers in high schools, and of young women in college and grad school so that they could take on leadership roles with greater confidence and ease.

I helped Kate take it a step further and articulate her social promise, which is to nurture the next generation of empowered, confident, and well-prepared female leaders. As a result of her social promise, Kate's business model has broadened, with a bigger reach to other sectors of society. She is feeling fulfilled and aligned with her purpose, passion, and her greater "why."

Kate is making more money now than ever before, and is on her way to making a meaningful social impact and creating her personal legacy, one day at a time.

CHAPTER SUMMARY

- Your life's purpose is as unique to you as your fingerprint. Essentially, your life's purpose is about accomplishing what fulfills you and gives your life meaning.

- You have a wonderful opportunity to express your passions and achieve your goals through your life's work.
- When you are aligned with your purpose, your work becomes an expression of your passions and of the contribution you want to make in the world.
- There are three main ways to discover your purpose and align it with your life's work: (1) Tap into your passion, because your passion leaves clues about what really fulfills you; (2) Reconnect with your greater "why" to gain clarity on the deeper meaning of your work; then align it with your money "why" to help anchor your connection to wealth; and (3) Create your purpose and impact statement.
- Since you are a spiritual being having a human experience, abundance is your natural state. Therefore, it takes more energy to resist this truth than it does to simply surrender, accept, and allow prosperity and success to flow to you.
- Social promise is about doing good while doing well in life. It includes a dual goal of combining wealth and profits with a mission to better society.
- Since for women money is about relationships, connections, and sharing, social promise and impact are a natural fit.

- If you are a business owner, you have the power to leverage your business to fuel your broader social promise and mission.
- Fulfilling your social promise can be expressed in many ways, such as giving back locally or globally to worthy causes and issues you care about most. There are many methods for doing so.
- Keep in mind that you do not have to wait to activate your social promise. And you do not have to own a business to express your social promise. You have the power now to shape how you want to make the world a better place.
- The act of tithing — giving and donating 10 percent, for example, of your income — is a spiritual practice that will bring more blessings and abundance into your life than you ever thought possible.
- Your social promise allows you to change lives and enrich your own life beyond your fondest dreams.

Take Action

Bonus download at:
www.MoneyManifestationAndMiracles.com/gift

Passion Treasure Quest

Chapter 12

Holistic Principle 6

IMPROVE YOUR MONEY HABITS AND ACTIONS

*When you want something, all the
universe conspires in helping you to achieve it.*
— PAULO COELHO

THROUGHOUT EACH OF THE CHAPTERS about the Eight
Holistic Principles you have been taking actions, with
the help of the various exercises and tips, to transform
and empower your relationship with money. Well done!

These actions have included the following:

- Gaining clarity of your strengths and personal
  values, and aligning them with the meaning of
  money.
- Shifting limiting beliefs and assumptions regarding money to ones that are more positive.
- Releasing and addressing emotional blocks to
  wealth.

- Expressing yourself and communicating about money in a more positive and optimistic way.
- Aligning your values, life's purpose, passion, and greater "why" with your life's work and money.

The focus of this chapter is on the holistic principle of action. Here you will continue your great momentum by taking further actions to shift your habits and actions with money to ones that are more productive and harmonious. By doing so you will become even more empowered with money. In this chapter, you will also be taking steps to create your new and more empowered money story. We will also go behind the scenes of what it really takes to manifest what you desire.

Aligning Your Money Habits and Actions

An essential way to improve your habits and actions with money is to develop integrity, self-responsibility, and accountability when it comes to wealth. Having integrity with your money happens on two levels — integrity with yourself and integrity with your actions.

Having integrity with yourself includes being in harmony with money. And as you know, when you are in alignment you will be able to put an end to any lingering self-sabotaging actions in relation to money that cause you to give away your power and decrease your self-confidence. This includes putting an end to underearning, overdelivering, undercharging, undervaluing your time and expertise, and having unclear boundaries, as discussed in chapter 9. Such actions stem from our innate nature as women to be nurturers and caregivers. They also come from wanting to be liked and to please others. As you are learning, when you love yourself, honor your worth, and are in alignment with your harmonious relationship with money, these patterns will begin to lessen.

Examples of being in integrity with your money can include the following:

- Paying your bills on time
- Using your money for your highest good
- Spending and handling money with care
- Earning money in an ethical and moral way

The second level of integrity relates to incorporating ethical practices into your life and work in relation to creating money and wealth. In other words, your efforts to earn money and prosper must also be directed by the highest degree of personal and business ethics. This also includes being mindful of how you spend, manage, save, and invest your money because how you think and feel about your money can determine how you treat it.

Make Money Your Best Friend

If money was your best friend, how would you treat it?

This may seem like a strange question. Yet you may be surprised to learn that money likes to be paid attention to. Money loves to be appreciated, respected, counted, spent, accumulated, flowing, spoken highly of, exchanged, and received. Money also likes to be around people who are powerful, people who are respectful, people who take action, and people who are open to receiving it. However, often we tend to do the opposite — we complain about money or hold on to it, limit its flow, speak about money in negative ways, or ignore it altogether.

Since money likes attention and wants to be treated with the same high integrity that you have in your other relationships, here are five simple tips to help you increase your money integrity and therefore the flow of money into your life:

Money Tip 1. Track all the money that comes into your life in addition to your income, including gift cards, birthday money, and more. This also includes your partner's income, bonuses, gifts, and so forth because it is all part of the abundance flowing into your life.

Money Tip 2. Track your spending to get an accurate picture of your profit and loss and where you are overspending.

Money Tip 3. Clean up any money areas that you may have neglected, such as missed payments or payments owed to you by your clients (if you are in business), repaying a friend or a relative, the bank, and so on.

Money Tip 4. Pay yourself first because that is part of putting yourself first. Regardless of the amount, it is important to pay yourself first.

Money Tip 5. You alone are responsible for your financial success. An example of taking responsibility with money includes addressing debt. There is good debt versus bad debt. Good debt relates to spending money on training and education, which is a necessary expense. Investing in yourself and in your growth is always a good investment. However, you must be sure to have a clear plan and schedule in place for repaying it in full. And you must consistently apply it.

Bad debt relates to amassing material goods that do not create lasting happiness and fulfillment and accumulating so much interest that it overwhelms you. This includes overspending while shopping, then blaming yourself afterward. A more constructive way to take responsibility is to get at the root of the behavior and the emotions related to the spending.

To create a greater flow of money in your work and life, you will need to:

- nurture a harmonious relationship with your money.
- align your personal integrity with your money integrity. If you are a business owner, you can align your business vision and mission with your highest standards, and deliver high-quality services and products.
- incorporate money as part of your ethical practices

(e.g., have clear boundaries, guidelines, and rules in place).

Create Your New Money Story

It is time to create your new, more empowered, and exciting money story!

Stories are one of the most ancient and widely used traditions that humankind has created. Throughout the centuries we have used stories to explain life events and to convey meaning. We understand ourselves through storytelling and seek data from our experiences to support our beliefs and story.

Your life is a story. The way you live tells a story about your identity, beliefs, hopes, triumphs, disappointments, desires, and dreams. Likewise, you also have a money story. Your money story is the subconscious and ongoing tale that you tell yourself about who you are, what money means to you, and what it says about you. It is a continuous dialogue about what and how much you deserve, what you are worth, what you are capable of, what you would do with more money, or what would happen if you lost it all.

Because of all the insights you have gained so far, you now have more clarity on your money story. You also have more clarity about what influences and shapes your money story. More important, you now know about the effects of your underlying feelings and beliefs regarding money.

A Bonus Tip

We make up stories as a way to explain our choices, both conscious and unconscious. Therefore, you also have the choice to change your story and create a different reality.

GWEN'S STORY

Gwen is an architect who owns a landscaping company. She has a mission related to nature and environmental conservancy.

She came to me wanting to create an expanded mission-driven business. When I asked her about her relationship with money, Gwen proceeded to tell me she found money to be a "hassle." Since she was a young child, she has thought that money just created too much drama, particularly as witnessed in the fights between her parents and extended family. Her father even declared personal bankruptcy at one point, which greatly affected her. Gwen vowed not to repeat this pattern. What she did instead was to avoid money as much as she could. Her bookkeeper and accountant take care of everything.

Gwen had been carrying around a disempowering money story for most of her life. It was obvious what a strong hold it had on her, because when I told her that she had the power to change her story and make a new beginning, she seemed bewildered.

However, she did take action by releasing her old story. In particular, she released the disempowering belief that she was a victim of her past circumstances. Then she was ready to create a new and more empowered money story about being at peace with money and being grateful for what money enabled her to do. She loved her new money story because it was powerful and positive.

The Gwen who showed up at the session after she wrote her new money story was a different person — more confident, more at ease, and happier. Moving forward, Gwen was able to fully step into the new identity of her empowered story. She felt in command and responsible for her financial success and abundance.

Fall in Love with Your Money Story

You now have a fresh opportunity to create your new money story as the CEO, leader, and hero of your life. This is the new money story you are setting as an intention to manifest into your reality. Your new money story will include your desired income. Remember that your current income represents your past — not your future. Thus, be sure to include an amount that is exciting, is a stretch, and would represent a financial breakthrough for you.

Here are six tips to keep in mind when writing your new money story:

Money Story Tip 1. Be specific about what changes you would like to see in your relationship with money. What will your work and life look like? Be specific about your goal(s). What will you specifically achieve, and by when?

Money Story Tip 2. Write your new story with you as the hero of your life.

Money Story Tip 3. Read your new story and assess how you feel. Are you excited about your story?

Money Story Tip 4. Assess what could get in the way of achieving your goals and what supports you will need in place to keep you on track.

Money Story Tip 5. Acknowledge yourself for creating a more empowered money story; celebrate all the steps and actions (big and small) to creating the reality you desire.

Money Story Tip 6. Read your money story every day to develop a strong connection to what you want to create. You can apply the manifesting tools discussed earlier in the book, including affirmations, meditation, creative visualization, and creating your ideal scene. You can also create a vision board to represent your story.

Now take a moment to write your new and empowered money story in your journal or on your computer. Then refer to it often.

Why Am I Not Getting What I Want?

You have been taking action by applying all the strategies and tips and by adopting more positive thoughts, beliefs, and emotions regarding money. And you are applying the Universal and Spiritual Laws of prosperity and abundance as well as the various manifesting tools. But what if you're still not seeing the results you desire?

There are likely various reasons for this, some of which we have explored in earlier chapters. Let's connect the dots even more here and examine the roles that these different factors can play in impeding our journey to abundance.

The Law of Attraction

As we know, the Law of Attraction operates on thoughts, emotions, words, and actions, which the Universe mirrors back to you through experiences. You must be in alignment with what you desire; you can only attract the people and circumstances that are on the same wavelength as you. Key ways to enhance your alignment are meditation, affirmations, and visualization.

Having said that, the Law of Attraction must be implemented properly. It is not enough to simply think and say what you want — and then do nothing else to achieve it. You must actively co-create your reality. This means that you must pay attention to the signs and opportunities that come your way, and take action.

Enhancing the Alignment

Before you can manifest money and more, everything must be in alignment. You can bring this about by thinking about and amplifying the feeling of what it is like to have money, amplifying the feeling of freedom, recognizing that you have options, recognizing that you can make a bigger impact, and more. When you amplify these feelings of flow, you will tap into the creativity and energy of the Universe and receive various ideas about attracting money into your life.

Keep in mind that you need to be clear on the "what" and the "why" and leave the "how" and "when" to the Universe. This is what Esther Hicks describes as "moving downstream" as opposed to moving upstream, where there is the energy of struggle. When you are moving downstream, you are allowing what you desire to manifest.

Affirmations

Affirmations are positive statements that help focus your awareness and energy on creating and having what you want.

In order for affirmations to work in your favor, you must use only those that feel appropriate for you and possible. If you are saying affirmations that deep down you do not believe or you think will be impossible to create, you will not get the results you want. For example, saying, "I now have $1 million," while not really believing you can have this sum because you're having trouble paying the bills, will be fruitless. This does not mean you cannot achieve this amount in the future when you truly believe it is indeed possible.

Intentions

Some people have difficulty, as I did many years ago, with understanding the difference between affirmations and intentions. An affirmation focuses on creating positive language and statements that, when said repeatedly with positive emotion, can create your reality. An intention is similar to a focused and directed goal. They complement each other in that affirmations can help support you in taking actions to achieve your intended goals.

Perhaps you are not getting what you desire because you are not clear enough about what you really want. Once you are clear about it, you must do whatever is necessary (within reason) to achieve it. Then you must surrender and release the outcome. This does not mean that you no longer care about it or that you forget about it. It simply means that you trust the Universe to do its work behind the scenes.

Gratitude

There is great power in being grateful for who you are, where you are, and what you have in the present moment. Gratitude opens your heart to receiving and giving blessings, thereby inviting even more opportunities for gratitude. Notice that when you feel grateful, your body is more relaxed, you are happier, and your personal energy operates at a higher level.

Conversely, when you focus on negative things, your body tenses up and your personal energy is lower. If you find yourself doing this, and noticing that you are not where you want to be with money, try practicing gratitude more often. Doing so will help you acknowledge your power and your ability to create. It will remind you that the Universe is truly abundant and that you can trust its rich flow into your life.

Prayer

A prayer is a direct communication between you and Divine Source and another way of expressing gratitude. Prayer is the moment when we allow the assistance of a more powerful force to be realized within us.

Given the Law of Attraction, it is important to pray from a place of love and possibility, such as: "I am grateful for…" rather than praying from a place of fear, such as, "I hope I don't lose my job" or "I really need to get some clients."

Remember that fear can be a magnet for negative energy, so you can attract what you fear. Just imagine the blessings and possibilities you can draw to you when you operate from a place of love and positivity.

The Power of Words

Any words that you repeat often enough can become true because they are operating as affirmations and declarations. Therefore, be extremely careful to choose words of wealth rather than scarcity. Our words and thoughts also carry an energetic force so be mindful of how you speak about money. A good practice to implement, before talking about money, is to first ask yourself, "Is this the experience I want?"

Patience

It is easy to become impatient when we don't see results right away. Creating and making a change is a process, and we need to be willing to allow the outcomes to manifest themselves.

When you plant a seed, you know that it will take time to grow into a flower. Although you cannot see it, you do not immediately stop believing that the flower will bloom. Instead, you nurture it and give it water and the proper sunlight and nutrients. Most of all, you believe that the flower will bloom in due time. The same idea applies when you are manifesting your goals and dreams into reality — you have to be patient, to trust, and to believe. Don't let impatience get in your way.

Residual Fear and Doubt

If you are not seeing the results you want, you may need to do more work on letting go of any residual fears and doubts that are blocking you from believing in yourself and your ability to create what you desire.

Examples of actions motivated by residual fear include putting off taking action; finding a new priority to keep you busy instead of working on what will move you forward; and attracting chaos into your life, which will divert your time, energy, and attention. Examples of actions motivated by residual doubt include falling back into unproductive old habits that keep you stuck, letting your Inner Critic stop you from taking action, and giving up and getting discouraged just when you are only a step or two away from accomplishing your dream.

Trust and Faith

Trust that your goals will bloom by detaching from the outcome. It is challenging when fears and doubts surface while you are in the process of creating what you want. This is natural. However, fear is actually misdirected energy that must be transformed into faith. Faith means preparing for the things you have asked for, even when there is no sign of their coming true.

Remember — you will receive what is for your highest good. This means that the exact outcome you desire may come about in a different way or at a different time than you imagined. From my experience, often the outcome is even better than what you imagined.

Environment

Make sure that your surroundings are not getting in your way. Your environment is very important, especially when you are in the process of creating a new reality. This includes being in the right physical environment, surrounding yourself with success-minded people, and much more. In some cases, it may be best to distance yourself from friends or even family members who have a negative outlook and do not help nurture your goals. We will discuss this in greater detail in chapter 13.

Enjoyment

Are you having fun? Or are you perhaps being too heavy about your money journey? You can gain the greatest freedom and satisfaction when you view the journey as fun and exciting instead of as a burden.

Ask yourself: "What can I do to enjoy the process?"

Accepting Abundance

We have briefly explored some of the factors that can get in the way of attaining what you want, especially when it comes to money. Let us now review four essential ingredients that can help you achieve financial prosperity and success: allowing success, letting go of resistance, letting money flow, and making the transition. They all relate to the action of acceptance, since you need to be in the right position to receive abundance. (You can download the complete Accepting Abundance exercise at the end of the chapter.)

Allowing Success

As you well know by now, where you are today has been influenced by your past choices and decisions. If you are not happy with the decisions you have made so far, then you can make different ones. This is all part of allowing success into your life.

You also need to feel good about what you do, since success comes from how you feel in the present moment. Some people may believe that only large sums of money will create that feeling for them. However, the truth is that many people with large sums of money do not necessarily feel successful, unless they have learned how to appreciate themselves and feel successful from within. You must feel prosperous and thrive on the inside before this state can be manifested on the outside.

Letting Go of Resistance

Throughout your journey, you have been letting go of certain beliefs, habits, and actions that have held you back and that no longer serve you. Consider this profound quote from Eckhart Tolle: "To offer no resistance to life is to be in a state of grace, ease, and lightness."

Letting go of any residual resistance to making more money is vital to your ability to move forward and develop money mastery. Remember that your current income represents your past, not your future.

Letting Money Flow

As you become more open to creating abundance, you will begin to recognize that money flows in and out. It is similar to the ebb and flow of ocean waves. There are times when money will come in and times when it will go out. This is also the case if you are in business for yourself. The challenge for entrepreneurs is not to permit the emotional ups and downs to affect them when money inevitably ebbs and flows.

The key is not only to release any blocks but also to align your personal energy with the energy flow of money. This includes raising your personal energy. Unblocking your energy in your physical body, your emotions, or your relationships with yourself, others, and money will enable you to create more wealth in your life.

Making the Transition

A wise woman once shared this great analogy with me. When you are in transition, it is like having the door to the past and the door to the future open at the same time. And you are caught in the draft between them. You have to decide. Where do I want to go next? Back to the past? Or forward to the future? You must be willing to close the door to the past so that you can move straight ahead toward the future. It can be scary walking through that door, but I know you can do it.

CHAPTER SUMMARY

- Throughout your journey, you have been breaking through and letting go of disempowering beliefs, habits, emotions, and actions regarding money. Well done!

- An important way to improve your habits and actions and to align them with money is to develop integrity, responsibility, and accountability when it comes to wealth. Having integrity with your money happens on two levels — integrity with yourself and integrity with your actions.

- It is time to create your new, exciting, and more empowered money story.

- You make up stories as a way to explain your choices, both conscious and unconscious. Therefore, you also have the choice to change your story and to fall in love with it.

- Your current income represents your past and not your future, so you can include a new story about the income that you desire.

- If you are not getting the results you want, there are likely various reasons for this, including not properly applying the Universal and Spiritual Laws of prosperity and abundance. This includes the practice of "offering no resistance to life."

- In order to allow more success and abundance into your life, you must first feel good about what you do and who you are.

- You can take action to accept more wealth and abundance in all areas of your life, including raising your personal energy.

- Remember, the more income you earn, the more lives you can improve and transform.

Take Action

Bonus download at:
www.MoneyManifestationAndMiracles.com/gift

Accepting Abundance Exercise

Chapter 13

Holistic Principle 7

EMPOWER YOUR GROWTH

Surround yourself only with people
who are going to take you higher.
— OPRAH WINFREY

WHEN YOU ARE ON A HIGH-GROWTH and transformational path with the intent of creating a life of prosperity, impact, and significance, you need support. Therefore, it is critical to surround yourself with the right environment. This includes being in an environment with success-minded people and communities that will truly support your growth and development.

Being in an environment of success also includes creating an optimal physical space to support your success. Additionally, there are environments that impact you on other levels — psychological, emotional, and spiritual

— which are also important to consider, since we cannot underestimate the effect of money on all areas of life.

In this chapter, our focus is on the holistic principle of environment. You will learn various tips and strategies to help you surround yourself with the best environment possible for your prosperity and success. Of course, there is also a temptation to try to do things on your own. It is admirable to have such determination, focus, and persistence. And while this might work for a while, I have personally found that the going-it-alone technique will not support you in the long term. Remember, "No (wo)man is an island."

We need these supportive people in our lives simply because it is impossible to see and address our own blind spots. And the continued existence of blind spots in our lives could hold us back from realizing the success we desire.

Take Your Success Higher

There are three essential areas related to creating an optimal environment for success (you can download the complete checklist at the end of the chapter):

1. Gaining a deeper understanding of the various environments that promote success, including psychological, emotional, spiritual, personal relationships, business, and physical
2. Getting clear on why these environments are so important to your success

3. Taking action to incorporate environment-related strategies into your work and life

Let us take a more detailed look at all the different environments that promote success.

Psychological Environment

When you think about your environment, the first thing that likely comes to mind is your physical and external environment. While physical environment is an important area and the most recognizable, you also need to consider your internal environment.

Since the effect of money shows itself in every area of your life, it is critical to explore your mind-set when putting the right environmental conditions into place. As we have discussed, everything starts with your mind-set, since it influences your beliefs, impacts your emotions, and affects your decisions and actions. Therefore, the quality of your mind-set, including your attitude toward money, is critical to your success.

The key action you can take to help you adopt an optimal mind-set is to nurture the state of "wealth consciousness" — a concept that is much broader than just generating money. It includes being grateful for who you are, what you have, and where you are on your journey. It also includes viewing life and the world as an abundant place where more opportunities are available to you than you can imagine.

Emotional Environment

There is power to your emotions, especially when it comes to money. As you know, your feelings influence not only your mind-set, decisions, and actions but also your beliefs. The emotions you have regarding money come from your beliefs about money. And since money is emotional currency for women, it is in your best interest to pay careful attention to your emotions regarding money. Ultimately, your relationship with your money is a reflection of your relationship with yourself — of how much you value, respect, and love yourself.

Spiritual Environment

As you now know, spirituality is a deep, soulful, and strong connection to God and Divine Source that you have access to at all times. There are many expressions of spirituality that you can practice, from praying to meditating to giving time and/or money to the causes you most care about.

Personal Relationships

We all need support on our life's journey. A vital component of your success is the quality of your relationships. It is a gift to have the support of your family and friends who love you, who believe in you and your dreams, and who support you through the highs and lows. I know that it has made a huge difference in my life to have such support.

As Jim Rohn once said, "You are the average of the five people you spend the most time with." Let us consider this statement in the context of your friendships. Do the friends and colleagues you spend the most time with have positive financial habits? If so, this will help you create an optimal social environment. However, if the people in your life feel disempowered with money, are fearful of spending, or create money drama and chaos, then you will need to reconsider whether you want to keep spending time with them.

Decide what type of friendships and networks you would like to have. It may not be easy to assess your existing friendships or reduce the amount of time you spend with certain friends. But spending less (or no) time with them does not mean you don't like them. Rather, it is about making choices not from the place where you are right now but from the place where you want to be as a successful woman and leader who is on a mission to make a meaningful impact on the world. Some factors you may want to consider in cultivating your friendships include being very honest and asking yourself:

- What am I getting from being friends with this person?
- Does the friendship simply exist because it is an old friendship?
- Do we still have anything in common, aside from the past?
- Even though the friendship is no longer fulfilling,

am I reluctant to break it off because I don't want
to hurt her or his feelings?

• Am I afraid to say no even when I really mean
  no?

EVA'S STORY

Eva is a copy editor and writer with a background in
graphic arts and marketing. Her business focuses on helping small businesses connect with their ideal audiences,
with pizzazz and originality, through their websites, promotions, and social media.

Eva left her corporate job in the advertising industry
after almost seven years. She connected with many great
colleagues there, including Natalie, who became a close
friend. Natalie was very supportive of Eva's big entrepreneurial leap and listened to all Eva's stories about her first
year. Yet regarding her own situation, Natalie admitted
to Eva that although she'd learned all that she could in
her job, she did not want to find something new because
"a job is a job." Natalie also complained about never having enough money and being late paying her bills and
even borrowed money from Eva on two occasions.

Even though Eva did well in her business right from
the start, she still commiserated with Natalie about not
having enough money coming in, so she could seem
like a supportive friend. But soon she tired of the com-
plaints. Eva started to expand her network to include
colleagues and friends of like-minded people who are

on the accelerated growth track. She began spending less time with Natalie. She stopped commiserating with her about not having enough money and strengthened her personal boundaries by saying no to Natalie when she asked to borrow some money. While she still liked Natalie, it became clear to Eva that they were at different levels of growth and had a different outlook on money and achieving success.

The process of surrounding yourself with the best people may mean letting go of people who are not aligned with you and your path. If you have friends that drain your energy, it is likely time to release them with love. It may not be easy, and it may take some time. However, when you do, it will be a turning point for you in realizing your growth, success, and transformation. Strengthening your personal boundaries is a vital part of moving forward more confidently.

Business Environment

To thrive in your work, you need to surround yourself with like-minded people who are part of a community of excellence. These are success-minded, goal-oriented people who can help take you higher because their successes will inspire and motivate you. They can serve as great role models, since you will have the opportunity to learn from how they handle challenges and setbacks, as well as successes. When you are part of a community of excellence, you can ask for support from coaches, mentors, and other professionals who can help you accelerate your growth in a way you could not do on your own.

My own entrepreneurial journey to success has included surrounding myself with this kind of community, one that is safe, trusting, respectful, fun, and full of the utmost integrity. My community of excellence includes high-level masterminds, top mentors, coaches, leaders, colleagues, and networks of talented, successful, and generous women and men. Being in such an environment has elevated my personal and professional growth in meaningful ways.

The mastermind concept was introduced by author Napoleon Hill in the early 1900s. Today this concept is embraced by many groups as a way to achieve respective goals and accelerate growth and success through brainstorming, accountability, and taking steps to move forward. In the book *Think and Grow Rich for Women*, Sharon Lechter credits the power of masterminding and brainstorming to her reframing the equation of $1+1=2$ to $1+1=11$. When you put yourself in a healthy environment, you will find that your colleagues will become your success partners, champions, and cheerleaders. They will be truly honest with you, hold you accountable, keep you focused, and pull you forward into the highest and best version of yourself. This is especially valuable in moments of doubt, fear, and challenge, which we all experience. And when money is an added layer, it can feel like an uphill battle toward success. You do not have to do it alone.

What this all comes down to is that in order for you to take yourself higher, you need to invest in yourself and your prosperous future. I truly believe the best investment we can ever make is in ourselves. This includes investing in yourself to:

- improve specific skills, including your money relationship.
- tap into your natural strengths and talents.
- enhance your credentials.
- increase your knowledge as a lifelong learner.
- transcend limitations and take focused actions from a place of certainty, confidence, and trust in yourself.

Investing in yourself and your future is the gateway to success. The results are powerful, profound, and life changing.

Physical Environment

Another vital aspect of taking your success to the next level is to create an uncluttered physical environment for yourself. Your physical space includes your home, closets, cabinets, office, wallet, and car. Your office space includes your cabinets, files (including electronic ones), work space, and desk, which we will discuss below.

Let me ask you this:

- When you look around your home, what does it say about you?
- Does your physical space, including your office, reflect who you are as a successful CEO and leader of your work and life?
- Does your overall physical space support the big money goal(s) you want to achieve?
- Does your physical space, particularly your office, support the energy of simplicity, beauty, and peace?

If you answered no to some or all of the questions above, then it's time to put your energy into creating a haven where you can surround yourself with beautiful things and create a feeling of harmony and peace.

A great way to achieve this feeling is by decluttering your physical space. A cluttered environment can perpetuate old, stagnated energy and work habits. This type of energy often attracts chaos, confusion, and even drama. And you definitely want the opposite of that!

When you declutter, you are making space for the new to come in. When there is a lot of clutter in your environment, there is no space for anything new to come in, including new ideas, new opportunities, new clients, and new resources. The energy simply cannot flow.

In fact, whenever I am feeling stuck and want to create or attract something new, including money, I clean out my filing cabinets and closets. The energy of releasing and letting go is invigorating. I do the same thing whenever I start a new project. In order to attract the new, you must release the old. Now it is your turn to assess your actual office space. Here are some tips to keep in mind:

Filing Cabinets: Are your documents in file folders? Is the cabinet organized, for example, in alphabetical order? And are you able to easily find and take out files?

File Folders: Are the file folders labeled? Are the files filled to the brim? Are the materials in the file folders still relevant?

Financial Documents: Do you have unopened bills that cause you to miss payments? What about monthly bank statements? Are your financial documents (contracts, receipts, invoices, bills) unsorted, hidden away in a filing cabinet, and not reviewed in years (rather than being sorted into folders)? Do you leave everything to your bookkeeper or accountant, remaining unaware of your numbers? Is the inside of your wallet messy with bills stuffed or folded?

If you answered yes to any of these, then you are not paying attention to your money, and your actions are contributing to creating financial clutter in your life. Having financial clutter blocks you from having clarity and stands in the way of having financial success because you are, in effect, pushing money away.

Electronic Files: You likely have more electronic files than you do physical ones. As such, decluttering files also includes your electronic files, emails, online subscriptions, text messages, and email lists. Delete the files you no longer require, and save the ones you do.

Shelves: Are the books in your office space just stacked on your desk in piles? Have they been there for a while? Are the books and magazines on your shelves still relevant and a crucial resource for your work or inspiration? If not, you can declutter this area and include only books and magazines that you need.

Desk: What items are on your desk, and do they belong there? Is your desk neatly organized or generally filled with papers, books, magazines, pens and pencils, and so on? One tip is to take five to ten minutes at the end of each workday to organize your desk and put things away, so you can start fresh the next day. A desk is an essential element of your work space, one that can be regarded as "sacred ground."

A Bonus Tip

The question to ask yourself when decluttering is: Will this book, article, or file serve me as a successful CEO and leader? If the answer is no, let it go.

Last, from the perspective of manifesting, when you take the time to create a more spacious environment, as well as set an intention for what you want, the Universe will fill it. This applies to all other areas of your life as well. Be aware that letting go of items in your physical space that no longer serve you can bring up emotions that you may need to release. Be gentle with yourself when this happens. I encourage you to try out these tips and be ready to welcome something new and magical.

CHAPTER SUMMARY

- Your environment is an important part of creating a new and successful reality.
- When you are on a high-growth, transformational path with the intent of creating a life of prosperity, impact, and significance, you will need support.
- It is vital to surround yourself with success-minded people who are positive, who believe in you and your dreams, and who have created the success you want to experience.
- You also need to immerse yourself in a community of excellence that is safe, fun, and goal-oriented and that will challenge you and pull you forward into the highest and best version of yourself.
- Other environments beyond the physical also impact you, including the psychological, emotional, and spiritual. Money affects all areas of our lives.
- Surround yourself with a physical environment of simplicity, beauty, and harmony because a cluttered environment can perpetuate old, stagnated energy — the opposite of what you want to create.
- If you want to attract new opportunities, let go of

things that no longer serve. In order to attract the new, you must release the old.

- If you are feeling stuck in some area of your life, including with money, perhaps it's time to declutter your physical environment and your relationships. This includes clearing the clutter in your office or home, as well as letting go of unsupportive and draining friendships and connections. It's time to make space for the things and the experiences you desire.

Take Action

Bonus download at:
www.MoneyManifestationAndMiracles.com/gift

Growth Empowerment Checklist

Chapter 14

Holistic Principle 8

FOCUS ON
ACHIEVING RESULTS

Act as if it were impossible to fail.
— DOROTHEA BRANDE

WE HAVE COME to the eighth and final holistic principle regarding transforming and empowering your relationship with money. All the holistic principles have been building on one other to help you promote harmony, balance, and flow with who you are and everything you do.

When you combine and effectively apply all the holistic principles, you will more easily generate the financial success you desire, as well as enduring wealth and abundance in all other areas of your life.

In this chapter, the focus is on helping you stay focused on your desired monetary goals. We will also explore tips for reaching your money goal, and finally, we will connect all Eight Holistic Principles with the Empowered Money Checklist. The complete version is available for download at the end of the chapter.

Keeping Your Eyes on the Prize

To achieve your money goals, you need to eliminate any distractions from your mind-set, from your interactions with others, and from your environment. It is essentially about making your goal your top priority and taking intentional actions.

Making your money goal your top priority involves releasing lingering resistances, including not getting carried away by fears, doubts, beliefs, and assumptions that can keep you distracted and unfocused. When you do become distracted, try to discern what kind of inner resistance your distraction stems from so that you can shift your attention away from it. You will then be able to carry on with your priority in a clear and focused manner.

If you do not make your goal a top priority and the focus of your attention, it will be nearly impossible to achieve. Thus, your ability to concentrate on achieving your goal is paramount. You can liken it to being an Olympic athlete and being very dedicated in your determination. While this may seem exaggerated, I have found that many success-minded people are easily distracted because they are highly creative and have millions of ideas. They can also end up losing focus on what they really want because life simply gets in the way. You are providing yourself a great service when you develop skills to help you focus.

Remember, "when you want something, all the universe conspires in helping you to achieve it." Yet this can only happen when you create the right conditions to make it happen. This includes co-creating your reality, prioritizing and focusing on what you desire, and not letting any opportunities pass you by.

We can all benefit from learning strategies to help us stay focused on our goals. Here are seven tips I created that you can adopt. You can also use these tips in other areas of your life beyond achieving your money goals.

Focus Tip 1. Eliminate any unnecessary distractions. Put aside other pursuits that are not priorities and can get in the way of achieving your goal.

Focus Tip 2. Schedule focused time to work on your goal. Time is such a precious resource because we can never get it back — so we must use it wisely. Managing your time effectively is critical to achieving your goal.

Focus Tip 3. Declutter by clearing away any material messes. This includes decluttering both in your living space and in your work space, as well as eliminating the items on your to-do list that are not priorities. You are creating space in your life for something new, including more money.

Focus Tip 4. This is a continuation of tip number 3. Create the best environment in which to thrive. Your physical environment must be in order. Having a clean and organized office will support your success. From a financial perspective, when papers are disorganized and you do not attend to your affairs, you can invite money chaos into your life. An example of this is when you forget to pay your bills, which can result in incurring late charges and losing money. It is basically a chain reaction of negative events.

Focus Tip 5. Practice self-care, including sleeping well, having proper nutrition, doing yoga, meditating, having quiet time, and getting exercise. Incorporate whatever you need to help you function at your very best. Keep in mind that your body is your best friend. It gives you signals through pain and discomfort. And it is your job to pay attention and make adjustments as needed.

Focus Tip 6. Stay committed to your goal, and apply the manifesting tools, including using affirmations, meditation, creative visualization, and creating your ideal scene. Any thoughts, images, or feelings that interfere with this or undermine your focus on your financial goals must be reframed and released, since they will only serve as obstacles to realizing your goals.

Focus Tip 7. Invest in your personal growth by working with a coach, mentor, another professional, or a mastermind group. You are your best resource, so you must do everything you can to get the right support in achieving your goals. It can be frustrating and isolating to make changes on your own, especially when trying to achieve big goals. No matter how organized and focused you are, you still need support.

While the support of family and friends is beneficial and needed, it cannot replace the specialized support you will need to accomplish your financial dreams and goals. This is why a professional coach or mentor is often necessary because he or she possesses the particular expertise, training, and skills to help you:

- gain clarity and greater self-confidence.
- navigate through challenges and blind spots.
- accelerate your personal growth, self-knowledge, and skills.
- accelerate your ability to achieve your overall vision, mission, and financial success.

TARA'S STORY

Tara is a former radio and local TV host who specializes in teaching presentation and vocal skills to entrepreneurs and leaders in corporations to get them "out of their shell" and find their authentic voice.

Tara knows herself well. She came to me to help her stay focused, committed, and accountable so she could increase her income without feeling overwhelmed and overworked. Although her team helped her, they of course still looked to Tara for leadership because she is the CEO.

Through the work we did together, Tara flourished

by setting and accomplishing meaningful goals, creating systems in her business so that things would run more smoothly, and increasing her income through additional lucrative revenue streams. All this has enabled her to enjoy a quality lifestyle with her husband and their daughter. Tara has also found time to volunteer at her daughter's school once a month, and she supports causes in her community.

Reaching Your Money Goals

Now that you have learned various strategies for staying focused, it is time to start putting them into action to achieve the big money goal you named and claimed in chapter 7.

Here is a list of seven money goal tips to keep in mind:

Money Goal Tip 1. Have a clear outcome in mind. What is the money for? And what will the money give you?

Money Goal Tip 2. Use the classic *SMART* criteria — make your goals *S*pecific, *M*easurable, *A*chievable, *R*ealistic, and *T*ime-based.

Money Goal Tip 3. Break a large goal into smaller steps and actions with key milestones so it does not feel overwhelming. You can also assess your goal every month and make adjustments as needed.

Money Goal Tip 4. Identify a process for regularly checking on your progress, and refine it as needed.

Money Goal Tip 5. Identify potential obstacles, including your Inner Critic, and incorporate ways to minimize them. Additionally, you will need to identify a way to hold yourself accountable.

Money Goal Tip 6. Post your goal and plan in a prominent spot so that they can act as daily reminders.

Money Goal Tip 7. Identify additional resources and supports that you may need to implement your plan, including the help of a professional coach, a mentor, or a mastermind group.

A Bonus Tip

You can also do this exercise every six to twelve months, or as needed. It is easier to break down goals in this time frame, since sometimes longer-term goals can seem too far in the future and less manageable.

Applying a Holistic Approach

You now have all the strategies, tips, and tools in place to help you achieve the financial prosperity, wealth, abundance, and success you desire. All the holistic principles have combined to help keep you in a place of alignment and harmony.

To further support you, I have created the Empowered

Money Checklist, which summarizes the key elements of the Eight Holistic Principles based on my Wealth Creation System. Each item on the checklist serves as a concise summary of the goal for each principle. You can refer to it daily as a resource and as a way to refresh your commitment to creating financial prosperity, success, and impact in your life. (You can download the complete one-page checklist at the end of the chapter for easy reference.)

Empowered Money Checklist

❏ I have a *clear understanding* of money and the personal meaning it holds for me in my life and work. This clarity will help me to stay true to my big money goals and to honor my self-worth.

❏ I have a *positive mind-set and attitude* toward wealth consciousness and use money as a tool to help me fulfill my highest potential and aspirations.

❏ I am committed to cultivating and nurturing *harmonious emotions* with money and will transform negative feelings regarding money into healthy emotional energy that will strengthen my pursuit of financial prosperity and success.

❏ I choose *optimal self-expression* regarding money and am committed to speak of money, wealth, and abundance in positive and healthy ways that raise the quality of my conversations about money.

❏ I am clear on my *greater purpose* and the *impact* I want to make on the world through my life's work, which guides the pursuit of my bold money goals. In turn, these goals are aligned with my overall life purpose, values, and mission.

❏ I will engage in *optimal actions* and habits regarding money, valuing myself and others in my goal to increase my financial prosperity. I will adhere to the highest level of personal and business ethics that values, respects, and empowers me and others.

❏ I will maintain the *best connections* and surround myself with the ideal environment in the firm belief that there is an unlimited supply of prosperity and abundance to meet my and everyone's financial and spiritual needs. Therefore, I fully accept my abundance now and let go of thoughts that undermine my conviction.

❏ I will develop *focus* and maintain clear attention on my money goals, directing my intention, energy, and actions solely toward achieving extraordinary results.

CHAPTER SUMMARY

• Each of the Eight Holistic Principles builds on the others — so that you can be in harmony, balance, and flow with who you are and everything that you do.

• In order to achieve your big money goal(s), it is vital to eliminate any unnecessary distractions from your mind-set, interactions with others, and environment. Essentially, it is about making your goal your top priority and then taking intentional actions.

- If you don't focus on your goal and make it a priority, it will be nearly impossible to achieve.
- Remember that "when you want something, all the universe conspires in helping you to achieve it." However, this only happens when you create the right conditions to make it happen. Therefore, you must actively co-create your reality.
- You now have all the strategies, tips, and tools in place to help you experience the financial prosperity, wealth, abundance, and success you desire.
- While the support of family and friends is beneficial and needed, it cannot replace the specialized support that you will need from a coach, mentor, other professional, or mastermind group to accomplish your financial dreams and goals.

Take Action

Bonus download at:
www.MoneyManifestationAndMiracles.com/gift

Empowered Money Checklist

CONCLUSION

You've always had the power.
— GLINDA, THE GOOD WITCH OF THE SOUTH,
IN *THE WIZARD OF OZ*

CONGRATULATIONS! You have achieved a huge milestone
in reading this book and applying the exercises, strategies,
and tools to transform your relationship with money.

You have embarked on a profound inner journey of
self-discovery, unlocking the nature of your unique relationship with money and ultimately your relationship
with yourself. This journey has also enabled you to unlock your riches, recognizing that the keys to abundance
have always been within you.

Through the Eight Holistic Principles, you now have
a more meaningful way to value yourself and honor your
worth. You also have a more meaningful way to create
wealth and prosperity in all areas of your life.

You have come full circle. Your journey has been a rite of passage — an awakening to reclaim your feminine connection to money as a source of empowerment, love, wealth, fulfillment, and success.

You are on an accelerated path to personal and spiritual growth as you take action to reach financial prosperity and success, while fulfilling your social promise in the world. Your pledge to improve the world can provide you with a motivation for aligning your purpose and passion with service and contribution.

It has been my pleasure to accompany you. What I know is that you are courageous for undertaking this inner journey. Remember that nurturing and strengthening your relationship with money is a lifelong commitment. As you continue, be sure to savor the journey and celebrate both the big and the small steps and achievements.

When situations arise that trigger your emotions regarding money, you now have a deeper understanding of the factors that shape your experiences. You also have the key tools to manifest your heart's desire with greater joy, grace, and ease. This book has guided you through a step-by-step system of creating a positive shift in your relationship with money as well as the way you think about and create money. Along the way, you may be tempted to cut corners to quickly get to your goals. But please don't skip any of the steps. Allow yourself to feel what you need to experience at each step of the way. Of course, you can take as much or as little time as you need within each step. And by taking all the steps, not skipping any, you will discover that success really is much, much sweeter when you savor the journey.

The seeds of prosperity and wealth have been planted and are being nurtured within you. As I conclude this book, I want to share with you the Fifteen Money Prosperity Tips so you always keep this easy reference and gentle reminder close at hand:

Money Prosperity Tip 1. Tap Into Your Power: You can feel inspired by the fact that whatever your past or current challenges with money are, they do not define who you are or dictate your future. You have the power to make intentional changes at this very moment. This can include letting go of your family's legacy with money so you can shape your destiny and create the prosperous life and future you desire.

Money Prosperity Tip 2. Nurture Your Money Relationship: Your relationship with money is as intimate as your relationship with yourself. The longest relationships you will have in your life are your relationship with yourself and your relationship with money. Like any important relationship, your relationship with your money must be nurtured.

Money Prosperity Tip 3. Money Reflects Every Area of Your Life: It is essential to understand what money means to you, how it functions in your life's work, and how it plays out in your life, in your relationships, and in your interactions with the world. This is because money is a mirror of other parts of your life. Everything is interrelated. What you do in one area of your life will impact another.

Money Prosperity Tip 4. You Can Have More: You can feel empowered with money right now. Prosperity and wealth are not something that other chosen people can have but you cannot. Feeling empowered with money is a matter of truly understanding who you are and what you want. It also includes not being afraid to ask for more. Women especially tend not to ask for what we want. Doing so does not come naturally to us. You must know that there is nothing wrong with wanting more. The truth is you can have more — as much as you are willing to receive.

Money Prosperity Tip 5. Keep Moving Forward: It takes courage to be financially prosperous. This is because you have to face your own shadows and fears regarding money, which can be uncomfortable. You may feel like walking away instead of addressing these shadows and fears. Money can certainly generate a lot of suppressed emotions, and you are called on to be very honest with yourself. This is a beautiful opportunity to make a huge breakthrough, so keep moving forward.

Money Prosperity Tip 6. Accept Abundance Now: It is within your power to create a harmonious, abundant relationship with money. Abundance is your natural state, so do not resist your good by adopting self-sabotaging patterns and actions. Instead, give in to the abundance that is available to you at this very moment.

Money Prosperity Tip 7. Use Money as a Tool for Success: Money is a tool for vitality and growth. It is the vehicle to help you realize your highest and fullest potential. You can align your money to your greater "why" and to your purpose. You can also leverage it to create a life of significance that makes a meaningful social impact.

Money Prosperity Tip 8. Release Residual Blocks to Wealth: Money is a physical manifestation of what you believe you deserve. As such, you can greatly benefit from releasing any limiting beliefs and emotional blocks to wealth. When you do, you become unstoppable in joyfully increasing your financial prosperity, success, and social impact on the world.

Money Prosperity Tip 9. You Are Worth It!: You have the ability to shift any disempowering emotions of fear, worry, or anxiety by actively choosing to feel worthy and deserving of all the prosperity and abundance that is available to you right now. Money is really more than just money. It is a reflection of your self-worth. Money is also a stand-in for what you really want — love, acknowledgment, recognition, happiness, success, and more.

Money Prosperity Tip 10. Incorporate a Holistic Approach to Wealth: Becoming prosperous also enables you to create true wealth in all areas of your life. Incorporating a holistic approach includes having a richness of love and joy in your relationships; vitality in your health and well-being; deep connection with Divine Source; passion for doing what you love; income to support your highest purpose and spiritual path; and a life of quality, meaning, and fulfillment.

Money Prosperity Tip 11. Live Your New Empowered Money Story: You can create a new and more empowered money story. The beautiful thing about stories is that you can change them at any time. Whatever you may have been telling yourself and others about money, you have the power to change that story right now. Remember that your current income represents your past and not your future, so you can include a new story about the income that you desire. Once you create your new money story, you can take actions to make it a reality.

Money Prosperity Tip 12. Prosperity and Wealth Begin with You: At the deepest soul level, you are the source of all your wealth, happiness, and abundance. The capacity to manifest your vision, dreams, and goals into reality resides in you. Everything begins with you. Manifesting money includes understanding and adopting various Universal and Spiritual Laws relating to financial prosperity, money, and abundance. It also includes taking inspired actions with which to create your reality. In other words, you must do the work!

Money Prosperity Tip 13. You Can Be Both Spiritual and Rich: You do not have to choose. You can be both. There is an unlimited supply of prosperity and abundance to meet everyone's financial and spiritual needs. No one is being deprived when you have what you need. Therefore, let your prosperity reflect the good you contribute to the world. In fact, the more money you earn, the more lives you can change for the better.

Money Prosperity Tip 14. Align Money with Your Social Promise: Since women are wired for relationships and connections, we can use money to express love — to take care of ourselves and others, to share it or give it away, and to help others. Money also provides security and experiences. Aligning money and social promise is a natural fit for women because a tremendous positive domino effect occurs when women are empowered with money. This effect can be profound and limitless because you can help your family, your community, the economy, and society while accomplishing the impact you want to make on the world.

Money Prosperity Tip 15. You Hold the Keys to Abundance: Mastering money is a wonderful inner journey of personal growth and enlightenment. You can become the best and highest version of yourself in the process. Once you understand the concept of wealth creation, you essentially hold the keys to abundance and can create money regardless of the state of the economy.

A Bonus Tip

Miracles follow when there is alignment between your highest self and your highest purpose, combined with taking inspired actions and implementing the Universal Laws. Collectively, these inspired actions create extraordinary results.

Your Call to Action

This is just the beginning for you on your journey to mastering money. As a woman on a mission, you have a tremendous opportunity to claim your wealth and rise as a force for good in the world. As you transform your relationship with money, you can:

- step into financial empowerment and experience emotional peace with money.
- create enduring wealth from within.
- achieve financial prosperity, fulfillment, and success on your terms; own your fullest worth; and express your brilliance.
- recognize your greatness and create a life of significance.
- generate a positive social impact through your life's work that uplifts humanity.

Imagine the possibilities...

Bonus Downloads

Download the exercises at:
www.MoneyManifestationAndMiracles.com/gift
and
download the Wealth Creation Assessment at:
www.MoneyManifestationAndMiracles.com/quiz.

*Pinpoint blind spots and identify solutions
for more financial prosperity.*

ACKNOWLEDGMENTS

THIS BOOK HAS HAD ITS OWN MONEY, manifestation, and miracles journey. I am grateful to the following people who, in their own way, supported its creation.

To Marc Allen and New World Library, my heartfelt thanks for your faith in me and my book.

A special thanks to Ingrid Vanderveldt for graciously writing the inspirational foreword. I am deeply honored to serve with you and empower women worldwide.

Many thanks to the following leaders and experts for their generous endorsements: Marc Allen, Sam Bennett, Cara Bradley, Kristine Carlson, Joy Chudacoff, Tania Gabrielle, Christine Hassler, Ruth Klein, Linda Page, Barbara Stanny, and Kendall SummerHawk.

To my dear colleagues and friends, thank you for

your support from the beginning: Robbin Simons, Mastery sisters, EBW sisterhood, OPS colleagues, Susan Brooks, Satya Kartara-Leighton, Lisa Watson, and Carol Vincent.

To my brilliant and courageous clients, thank you for your vulnerability and authenticity. It is a privilege to work with you and see you flourish and thrive.

Thank you to my parents, Roque and Elisa Manrique; my sisters, Maricon, Gia, and Maricia; and my extended family, for your unwavering support and encouragement throughout my life's journey.

To my dynamic daughter, Alexa, you are a blessing. Thank you for enriching my life.

Finally, to my husband and champion, Tony, thank you for your love, patience, and wisdom.

NOTES

Page 3, *add $12 trillion to global economic growth by 2025*: Jonathan Woetzel et al., "How Advancing Women's Equality Can Add $12 Trillion to Global Growth," McKinsey Global Institute, report, September 2015, www.mckinsey.com/global-themes/employment-and-growth /how-advancing-womens-equality-can-add-12-trillion-to-global -growth.

Page 4, *if women were to attain full gender equality*: Kweilin Ellingrud et al., "The Power of Parity: Advancing Women's Equality in the United States," McKinsey Global Institute, report, April 2016, www.mckinsey.com/global-themes/employment-and-growth/the -power-of-parity-advancing-womens-equality-in-the-united-states.

Page 4, *an extra £150 billion*: Vivian Hunt et al., "The Power of Parity: Advancing Women's Equality in the United Kingdom," McKinsey Global Institute, report, September 2016, www.mckinsey.com /global-themes/women-matter/the-power-of-parity-advancing -womens-equality-in-the-united-kingdom.

Page 4, *could lead to $92 billion in GDP*: "Gender Parity Improves

Profitability, Workplace Culture and Benefits the Economy at Large
— PwC Report," *Cision*, 2016, www.newswire.ca/news-releases
/gender-parity-improves-profitability-workplace-culture-and
-benefits-the-economy-at-large---pwc-report-597489321.html; see
also "Women in Work Index 2017: The Potential $2 Trillion Prize
from Closing the Gender Pay Gap," *PwC*, report, www.pwc.co.uk
/services/economics-policy/insights/women-in-work-index.html.

Page 4, *"Some people may call me a feminist"*: Dalailamacenter.org/blog
-post/reflections-women-and-peace-building; see also Amy O'Brian,
"'We Need More Effort to Promote Basic Human Values': Dalai
Lama," *Vancouver Sun*, September 27, 2009, www.vancouversun
.com/touch/need+more+effort+promote+basic+human+values
+dalai+lama/2039661/story.html?rel=2041171.

Page 4, *more effectively benefit from financial literacy*: "Measuring Financial Literacy: Questionnaire and Guidance Notes for Conducting an
Internationally Comparable Survey of Financial Literacy," OECD,
report, October 2011, www.oecd.org/finance/financial-education
/49319977.pdf.

Page 5, *Many great resources for women*: For example, www.worthfm
.com; www.dailyworth.com; www.learnvest.com; and www.ellevest
.com.

Page 6, *Women control $39.6 trillion*: Megan Leonhardt, "Women's
Wealth Growing Faster Than Men's," *Money* magazine, June 7,
2016, time.com/money/4360112/womens-wealth-share-increase.

Page 6, *190 female billionaires worldwide*: Bartie Scott, "The Richest
Women in the World," *Forbes* magazine, March 1, 2016, www
.forbes.com/sites/bartiescott1/2016/03/01/the-richest-women-in-the
-world-2016/#1771ed921667.

Page 6, *Women control more than 60 percent*: Ekaterina Walter, "The
Top 30 Statistics You Need to Know When Marketing to Women,"
TNW, January 24, 2012, thenextweb.com/socialmedia/2012/01/24
/the-top-30-stats-you-need-to-know-when-marketing-to-women
/#.tnw_3pDOpEwW.

Page 6, *51 percent hold doctoral degrees*: Bridget Brennan, "Why Has
Women's Economic Power Surged?: Five Stats You Need to Know,"

Forbes magazine, January 31, 2017, www.forbes.com/sites/bridge
tbrennan/2017/01/31/why-has-womens-economic-power-surged
-five-stats-you-need-to-know/#3925a3d99562.

Page 6, *40 percent of women are the primary or sole*: Brennan, "Why
Has Women's Economic Power Surged?," www.forbes.com/sites
/bridgetbrennan/2017/01/31/why-has-womens-economic-power
-surged-five-stats-you-need-to-know/#3925a3d99562.

Page 6, *70 percent of women with children*: Brennan, "Why Has Women's
Economic Power Surged?," www.forbes.com/sites/bridget
brennan/2017/01/31/why-has-womens-economic-power-surged
-five-stats-you-need-to-know/#3925a3d99562.

Page 7, *global incomes of women are predicted*: "Women: The Next
Emerging Market," EY report, n.d., www.ey.com/Publication
/vwLUAssets/Women_the_next_emerging_market/$FILE
/WomenTheNextEmergingMarket.pdf.

Page 7, *Women control 85 percent*: Walter, "Top 30 Statistics," the
nextweb.com/socialmedia/2012/01/24/the-top-30-stats-you-need
-to-know-when-marketing-to-women/#.tnw_3pDOpEwW.

Page 7, *running established businesses*: Donna J. Kelley, Candida G. Brush,
Patricia G. Greene, and Yana Litovsky, "Global Entrepreneurship
Monitor 2012 Women's Report," GEM, 2012, www.babson.edu
/Academics/centers/blank-center/global-research/gem/Documents
/GEM%202012%20Womens%20Report.pdf.

Page 7, *In Canada 15 percent*: "Key Small Business Statistics: June 2016,"
Innovation, Science and Economic Development Canada, report,
June 2016, www.ic.gc.ca/eic/site/061.nsf/vwapj/KSBS-PSRPE
_June-Juin_2016_eng.pdf/$FILE/KSBS-PSRPE_June-Juin_2016
_eng.pdf.

Page 7, *1,072 (net) new women-owned firms launched*: "The 2016 State of
Women-Owned Businesses Report," American Express OPEN, re-
port, April 2016, www.womenable.com/content/userfiles/2016
_State_of_Women-Owned_Businesses_Executive_Report.pdf.

Page 7, *five times the national average*: "The 2016 State of Women-Owned
Businesses Report," www.womenable.com/content/userfiles/2016
_State_of_Women-Owned_Businesses_Executive_Report.pdf.

Page 8, *generating more than $1.6 trillion in revenues*: "The 2016 State of Women-Owned Businesses Report," www.womenable.com/content /userfiles/2016_State_of_Women-Owned_Businesses_Executive _Report.pdf.

Page 8, *starting and growing successful businesses*: Joanna Smith, "Justin Trudeau, Donald Trump Team Up to Support Women in the Workforce," *Global News*, February 13, 2017, Globalnews.ca /news/3246085/donald-trump-justin-trudeau-women-in-work force-a-boost-for-economic-growth.

Page 8, *women earn 77 cents*: "Press Release: Activists, Celebrities and Governments Call to End Global Gender Pay Gap," UN Women, press release, March 13, 2017, www.unwomen.org/en/news/stories /2017/3/press-release-activists-celebrities-and-governments-call-to -end-global-gender-pay-gap.

Page 8, *women earn 87 cents*: Solomon Israel, "StatsCan on Gender Pay Gap: Women Earn 87¢ to Men's $1," *CBS News*, March 8, 2017, www.cbc.ca/news/business/statistics-canada-gender-pay-gap -1.4014954.

Page 9, *women earn 9.4 percent less*: Patrick Scott, "International Women's Day 2017: How Big Is the Gender Pay Gap Where You Live?," *Telegraph*, March 8, 2017, www.telegraph.co.uk/news/2016/10/26/uks -gender-wage-gap-narrows-to-record-low-how-does-it-fare-where.

Page 9, *women earn 79 cents*: Sonam Sheth and Skye Gould, "5 Charts Show How Much More Men Make Than Women," *Business Insider*, March 8, 2017, www.businessinsider.com/gender-wage-pay-gap -charts-2017-3.

Page 10, *the percentages are higher in Europe*: "Women on Corporate Boards Globally," Catalyst, report, March 16, 2017, www.catalyst .org/knowledge/women-corporate-boards-globally.

Page 10, *nine as heads of government around the world*: "Facts and Figures: Leadership and Political Participation," UN Women, report, July 2017, www.unwomen.org/en/what-we-do/leadership-and-political -participation/facts-and-figures.

Page 10, *21 percent of the Senate*: "Women in Government," Catalyst,

report, February 15, 2017, www.catalyst.org/knowledge/women
-government.

Page 10, *43 percent of the Senate*: "Women in Government," www.catalyst
.org/knowledge/women-government.

Page 10, *26 percent of members in the House of Lords*: "Women in Parliament and Government," House of Commons Library, July 12, 2017,
researchbriefings.parliament.uk/ResearchBriefing/Summary
/SN01250.

Page 10, *imbalanced share of family work, and a lack of self-confidence*:
Emily Fetsch, Chris Jackson, and Jason Wiens, "Women Entrepreneurs Are Key to Accelerating Growth," Ewing Marion Kauffman
Foundation, report, July 20, 2015, www.kauffman.org/what-we-do
/resources/entrepreneurship-policy-digest/women-entrepreneurs
-are-key-to-accelerating-growth; see also Kiera Abbamonte, "Wom-
en's Entrepreneurship: 2017 State of Women in Business," *Entrepreneurship, Women & Business*, March 7, 2017, grasshopper.com/blog
/womens-entrepreneurship-2017-state-of-women-in-business.

Page 10, *use personal savings for capital*: Alicia Robb, Susan Coleman, and
Dane Stangler, "Sources of Economic Hope: Women's Entrepreneurship," Ewing Marion Kauffman Foundation, report, No-
vember 2014, http://www.kauffman.org/~/media/kauffman_org
/research%20reports%20and%20covers/2014/11/sources_of
_economic_hope_womens_entrepreneurship.pdf.

Page 11, *a share that has not changed during the past twenty years*: "The
2016 State of Women-Owned Businesses Report," www.womenable
.com/content/userfiles/2016_State_of_Women-Owned_Businesses
_Executive_Report.pdf.

Page 11, *despite generating $1.6 trillion in revenues*: "The 2016 State of
Women-Owned Businesses: Summary Tables," www.womenable
.com/content/userfiles/2016_State_of_Women-Owned_Businesses
_Summary_Tables.pdf.

Page 25, *"After you become a millionaire"*: "Jim Rohn Quotes," Mind of
Success, www.mindofsuccess.com/jim-rohn-quotes/.

Page 40, *never completely stop worrying about it*: "The Brilliant Mind

behind *Harry Potter*," Oprah.com, www.oprah.com/oprahshow
/the-brilliant-mind-behind-harry-potter.

Page 48, *women control 85 percent*: Walter, "Top 30 Statistics," thenext
web.com/socialmedia/2012/01/24/the-top-30-stats-you-need-to-know
-when-marketing-to-women/#.tnw_3pDOpEwW.

Page 144, *women in the United States fear*: "Despite More Financial Control, Women Still Fear Becoming a 'Bag Lady,'" Allianz, report,
2013, www.allianzusa.com/retirement/retirement-insights/women
-money-and-power-study.

Page 163, *rock bottom became the solid foundation*: J. K. Rowling, "The
Fringe Benefits of Failure, and the Importance of Imagination,"
Harvard Gazette, speech at Harvard University, June 5, 2008,
news.harvard.edu/gazette/story/2008/06/text-of-j-k-rowling-speech.

Page 176, "Should *is one of the most damaging words*": Louise L. Hay,
Experience Your Good Now: Learning to Use Affirmations (Carlsbad,
CA: Hay House, 2010), 30.

Page 193, *women reinvest 90 cents of every dollar*: Sadaffe Abid, "The
Female Economy," *Express Tribune*, opinion, June 30, 2016, tribune
.com.pk/story/1133665/the-female-economy.

REFERENCES

Allen, Marc. *The Millionaire Course: A Visionary Plan for Creating the Life of Your Dreams.* Novato, CA: New World Library, 2003.

Brizendine, Louann. *The Female Brain.* New York: Harmony, 2006.

Brown, Brené. *The Gifts of Imperfection: Let Go of Who You Think You're Supposed to Be and Embrace Who You Are.* City Center, MN: Hazelden, 2010.

Carson, Rick. *Taming Your Gremlin: A Surprisingly Simple Method for Getting Out of Your Own Way.* New York: William Morrow, 2003.

Chopra, Deepak. *The Seven Spiritual Laws of Success: A Practical Guide to the Fulfillment of Your Dreams.* Novato, CA: New World Library, 1994.

Coelho, Paulo. *The Alchemist.* San Francisco: HarperOne, 1993.

Cooper, Diana. *A Little Light on the Spiritual Laws.* Moray, Scotland: Findhorn, 2007.

Gawain, Shakti. *Creative Visualization: Use the Power of Your Imagination to Create What You Want in Your Life.* Novato, CA: New World Library, 2002.

Haidt, Jonathan. *The Happiness Hypothesis: Finding Modern Truth in Ancient Wisdom*. New York: Basic, 2006.

Hicks, Esther, and Jerry Hicks. *Ask and It Is Given: Learning to Manifest Your Desires*. Carlsbad, CA: Hay House, 2004.

Krueger, David, and John David Mann. *The Secret Language of Money: How to Make Smarter Financial Decisions and Live a Richer Life*. New York: McGraw Hill, 2009.

Lechter, Sharon. *Think & Grow Rich for Women: Using Your Power to Create Success and Significance*. New York: Tarcher/Penguin, 2014.

Levinson, Kate. *Emotional Currency: A Woman's Guide to Building a Healthy Relationship with Money*. Berkeley, CA: Celestial Arts, 2011.

Mackey, John, and Rajendra Sisodia. *Conscious Capitalism: Liberating the Heroic Spirit of Business*. Boston: Harvard Business Review Press, 2014.

Roman, Sanaya, and Duane Packer. *Creating Money: Attracting Abundance*. Novato, CA: New World Library, 2007.

Sandberg, Sheryl. *Lean In: Women, Work, and the Will to Lead*. New York: Knopf, 2013.

Stanny, Barbara. *Overcoming Underearning: A Five-Step Plan to a Richer Life*. New York: HarperBusiness, 2007.

Tolle, Eckhart. *The Power of Now: A Guide to Spiritual Enlightenment*. Novato, CA: New World Library, 1999.

Twist, Lynne. *The Soul of Money: Reclaiming the Wealth of Our Inner Resources*. New York: Norton, 2003.

ABOUT THE AUTHOR

MERIFLOR TONEATTO is an award-winning leadership and coaching executive, entrepreneur, speaker, and author. She is the founder and CEO of Power With Soul Inc. and creator of the Millionaire Difference Makers Path™ and the Wealth Creation System — a holistic approach to creating wealth and prosperity in all areas of life.

Combining her twenty-year leadership, business, and social-impact experience with expertise on women and money, Meriflor specializes in helping ambitious women entrepreneurs, professionals, and leaders internationally reach financial prosperity and fulfill their social promise. Her programs and trainings empower women to thrive, flourish, and rise as a force for good in business and life.

Meriflor holds postgraduate designations in professional coaching and is a professional certified coach. She also holds a bachelor's degree in social policy and management and is pursuing a master's in positive psychology and coaching psychology.

She lives with her family and their lovable golden retriever in Toronto, Canada.

To learn more, please visit www.Meriflor.co.

NEW WORLD LIBRARY is dedicated to publishing books and other media that inspire and challenge us to improve the quality of our lives and the world.

We are a socially and environmentally aware company. We recognize that we have an ethical responsibility to our customers, our staff members, and our planet.

We serve our customers by creating the finest publications possible on personal growth, creativity, spirituality, wellness, and other areas of emerging importance. We serve New World Library employees with generous benefits, significant profit sharing, and constant encouragement to pursue their most expansive dreams.

As a member of the Green Press Initiative, we print an increasing number of books with soy-based ink on 100 percent postconsumer-waste recycled paper. Also, we power our offices with solar energy and contribute to non-profit organizations working to make the world a better place for us all.

Our products are available in bookstores everywhere.

www.newworldlibrary.com

At NewWorldLibrary.com you can download our catalog,
subscribe to our e-newsletter, read our blog,
and link to authors' websites, videos, and podcasts.

Find us on Facebook, follow us on Twitter, and watch us on YouTube.

Send your questions and comments our way!
You make it possible for us to do what we love to do.

Phone: 415-884-2100 or 800-972-6657
Catalog requests: Ext. 10 | Orders: Ext. 10 | Fax: 415-884-2199
escort@newworldlibrary.com

NEW WORLD LIBRARY
publishing books that change lives   14 Pamaron Way, Novato, CA 94949